LIVING BETTER
WITH YOURSELF

LIVING BETTER WITH YOURSELF

A Practical Guide to Embodied Growth

MICHAEL CONTI

The Horse's Mouth

Published in Søborg, Denmark, by The Horse's Mouth

ISBN: 978-87-973123-0-8

Important Note
This book is not intended as a substitute for medical advice or treatment. Any person with a condition requiring medical or therapeutic attention should consult a qualified medical practitioner or suitable therapist.

Book design and illustrations by Michael Conti
Audio production by Michael Conti
Editing and proof-reading by Lewis John Greenslade
Image on p. 40 adapted from dreamstime.com/legger

Audio files can be streamed or downloaded for personal use only from:
thehorsesmouth.michaelconti.net/lbwy-audio

thehorsesmouth.michaelconti.net

TABLE OF CONTENTS

LIST OF EXERCISES

CHAPTER 07 – On Fear

CHAPTER 08 – On Being Angry

CHAPTER 09 – On Shame and Guilt

CHAPTER 10 – On The Inner Critical Voice

CHAPTER 11 – On 'Should' Statements

CHAPTER 12 – On Control

CHAPTER 13 – On Being Good and Not-So-Good

~ 01 ~

PLEASE DON'T SKIP ME

This isn't just another self-help book. Instead, it adopts a more holistic and embodied approach towards self-development. It gives particular importance to how we can use our body to better our understanding of ourselves and further our personal growth. Through a series of texts and exercises, this book will help you to integrate your body, emotions, thoughts, behaviour and past experiences. In doing so, it offers you the opportunity to deepen your self-awareness and address aspects of growth and healing.

This book isn't made to sit beautifully on your bookshelf. It isn't just intended to be read. That's why there's space for you to scribble down your thoughts and reflections, to draw and to take note of any lessons you learnt while working through the exercises. When you reach the end of it, it will hopefully bear signs of wear and tear. It needs to have become part of you! Feel free to copy the parts of this book that you can write on so that you repeat the exercises multiple times. Should you prefer not to write on this book or if you are using an eBook version, use a notebook for your journalling. But don't just buy any notebook – buy a beautiful one as it will be bearing witness to your personal growth!

The first section looks at some fundamental aspects of ourselves. First we talk about the role that our body, mind and emotions play in our life and the way they relate to each other. This is accompanied by some exercises aimed at helping you deepen your general connection with your body, emotions and thoughts. These exercises can be used in combination with others throughout the rest of the book. We also look at how our behaviour and our past are woven into the fabric of who we are today and how we change. We briefly talk about what it means to be a relational being and the experience of what lies beyond our sense of self. In the last part of this section, we take a closer look at stress, how we deal with it through the stress response and how stress can develop into trauma.

The second section explores some of the major themes that people struggle with in life on a personal level. Each chapter deals with a specific issue and starts with a brief introduction. This isn't designed to provide you with an extensive explanation on the matter. Instead, it offers a key insight into the issue and sets the context for the exercises that follow. The exercises are the main component of the book. They are what will help you start bringing about some of the change that you desire in your life.

The book you hold in your hands is not intended to be read in one go. It's more like a reference book than a novel. Select the chapters that you feel are more relevant to you at this particular moment in your life. Pause your reading as often as necessary in order to digest what you're taking in and to reflect on how it relates to your life. Focus on what you need and come back multiple times to chapters and exercises that you find helpful.

Some of the exercises are marked with a sound icon. These exercises include audio files that can be streamed or download from: **thehorsesmouth.michaelconti.net/lbwy-audio.**
The links for the audio for each chapter can also be found at the beginning of each chapter, together with a QR code that can be scanned by mobiles or tablets to take you directly to the link.

A lot of the exercises are arranged in a way that they build upon each other, offering you a gradual path towards your own development. This will guide you through a process that first increases your current awareness around that particular area in your life. From there, it will aid you in better understanding how your past contributed in the process and, finally, it will provide you with ways to help you further develop that area in your life.

There might be, however, some exercises that you don't feel comfortable carrying out or they may not be appropriate for you in this particular moment in life. There's no expectation that you complete all of the exercises and skipping one of them doesn't mean that you're compromising your development. So, only engage with the exercises you feel comfortable carrying out, but also make sure that you're challenging yourself enough by gently stepping outside of your comfort zone. Otherwise, no growth will take place!

Personal growth isn't an easy process. There may be times when you feel glad or surprised about what you've learnt about yourself. Other times you might experience a strong sense of emotional release. However, some exercises can also bring up upsetting thoughts, emotions or memories. This is because, when we embark upon a process of growth, we disturb the state of how things have been inside us for a long time. We disturb the status quo that we've become used to. It's like trying to clean a muddy lake – the moment we start dredging the mud from the bottom of the lake, the water turns all dirty and brown. But it's only by doing so that we can really clean it out! So, if you start experiencing upsetting thoughts, emotions or memories, don't be alarmed – it's normal for this to happen.

However, if this becomes very upsetting for you, and especially if it brings up feelings or memories that are particularly difficult to deal with, it's advisable to seek the help of a professional who's trained to work with such issues. Doing so can offer you additional support that, at times, is necessary in order to heal what's causing you the pain. Such support may also help you integrate what you learn from this book into your life even more.

Now it's time to take the courageous leap. Allow yourself to be curious. Get to know yourself better and grow further.

All the exercises that have this sound icon include an audio file that can be streamed online or downloaded for your personal use only. At the beginning of each chapter, you will find a link to access the audio files and a QR code that you can scan. In the case of eBooks, the icons are a direct link to the online audio file.

The audio files can be streamed or downloaded from **thehorsesmouth.michaelconti.net/lbwy-audio** *or by scanning the adjacent QR code.*

OUR SELVES

02

OUR BODY

Bring to mind the image of a coin. If you have one close by, hold it in your hand. Take note of its head side. Flip it over and look at the tail side. Where does the head stop and the tail begin? Is the coin separate from the head or the tail? Can you have a head or a tail without there being a coin?

We can think of our body, thoughts and emotions in a similar way. Our thoughts and emotions are like the head and the tail. They exist together – one cannot exist without the other, but they're both different aspects of ourselves. Our body, like the coin, holds them all together. In the same way that we cannot separate the head and the tail from the coin, our emotions and thoughts cannot be separated from our body. And in the same way that the head and the tail are expressions of the coin's body, our thoughts and emotions are both expressions of our body and have the power to shape it. After all, without our body, we don't exist.

Audio files for this chapter can be accessed at **thehorsesmouth.michaelconti.net/lbwy-ch02** *or by scanning the adjacent QR code.*

And yet, we often discount our body. We don't give it the importance it deserves or we focus on some of its aspects and ignore its link to our emotions and thoughts. We see it as something separate. But our body is us, as much as our emotions and thoughts are.

Our emotions and thoughts affect what happens in our body. If we're feeling sad or helpless, we tend to slouch and look down. If we're anxious, our eyes dart around, we get fidgety and we might even have bowel problems. If we're angry, we can tense our muscles, make fists with our hands, hit something or experience tightness in our chest. If we try hard to remember something, we frown.

Because our body is so intimately linked to our emotions and thoughts, when these are very strong, they can end up being stored in our body. This is particularly the case with traumatic situations where our body remembers the trauma even though our consciousness might have 'forgotten' it.

The opposite is also true. Our body affects our emotions and our thinking. If we clench our fists for some time, we start feeling some anger. If we get a massage, we feel relaxed and we stop worrying for a while. If we exercise, we feel more energetic. If we're always slouched, it will lower our confidence. Hence, our emotions, thoughts and body are constantly affecting each other.

The first step towards being happier with oneself is to accept how we feel, what we think and how our body behaves without judging these as being right or wrong. Only then can we use our emotions, thoughts and body to bring about the change that we desire in our lives.

When we struggle with our emotions or thoughts, we often try to change them directly. If we're feeling sad, we try to think of positive things. If we feel anxious, we try to examine our thoughts and emotions in order to understand why we're feeling that way. If we worry too much, we try to think differently. This can be very helpful at times, but sometimes we still don't succeed in bringing about the change we desire. The reason for this is that we're attempting to use parts of our mind to control other parts of our mind. But our mind knows itself much better than we do and so it's very difficult to trick it or to control it. When this happens, it's best to focus on our body as a means to sidestep the complicated distortions our mind can create.

The following are some fundamental exercises to help you increase your awareness of your body and your ability to use this to change your emotions, thoughts and behaviour. In the rest of the book, you will encounter additional exercises that focus on your body in relation to specific topics. Remember to choose which exercises you feel are relevant to you rather than just going from one to the next.

Breathing

Breathing activates the core of our torso, a place where we store many emotions. Many of us tend to breathe quite shallowly using primarily the upper chest. Some of us take deeper breaths and engage the diaphragm more. The deeper we breathe, the better we connect to our body. The deepest kind of breathing can be achieved by trying to breathe right down to our anus, thus engaging the whole torso and activating different energy centres in our body. The following are some breathing techniques that you can practise on your own. Some of them are geared more towards relaxing the body, while others are geared more towards activating it.

01. *Square breathing*

This breathing technique helps you achieve a general sense of relaxation and can be especially useful before sleeping. Breathe gently and feel free to change the duration of the counting to suit your needs.

- Inhale counting to 4.
- Hold your breath for a count of 4.
- Exhale counting to 4.
- Pause between breaths for a count of 4.

02. *4-7-8 breathing*

This breathing technique helps you achieve general relaxation.

- Exhale slowly and completely through your mouth.
- Inhale quietly and deeply through your nose counting to 4.

- ✆ Hold your breath for a count of 7.
- ✆ Exhale slowly and completely through your mouth for a count of 8.

03. *Hollow body breathing*

This breathing technique helps you to achieve a sense of being present in the here-and-now and to connect more to the inside of your body.

- ✆ Imagine your body as a hollow cavity.
- ✆ Inhale through your nose and imagine that your breath is flowing into your hollow head. Imagine the air whirling inside it, caressing the insides of your head.
- ✆ Exhale through your mouth. Imagine the air leaving your head and feel it flow out through your mouth.
- ✆ Take each body part in sequence from the top of your head to your toes and repeat this process. Each time, imagine the air flowing into and out of each different part of your body.
- ✆ Finally, take a few breaths while imagining the air flowing into your whole body in one go.

04. *Anal breath*

This technique helps you achieve a strong sense of grounding and activates a part of the body that some of us give less attention to. It also helps strengthen the pelvic floor muscles which support your bladder and bowels and are important in sexual activity.

- ✆ You might find it easier to do this exercise while being on your knees and elbows. This allows you to notice more the contractions of your anus and makes the chest feel lighter. If this position is uncomfortable for you, sit on a chair with your back slightly arched so that you can feel the inside of your bum slightly more exposed.

- ꙮ Clench your anus tightly while you start breathing in, imagining that the air is being sucked up by your anus and travelling through your mouth and torso, all the way up to your anus. Notice how you become aware of the inside of your pelvis in the process.
- ꙮ When you exhale, relax your anus and let go of all pressure in your torso.

05. *Lion's breath*

This breathing technique energises you and relieves tension from the chest and face.

- ꙮ Sit comfortably and press your palms down against your knees with your fingers spread wide.
- ꙮ Inhale deeply through your nose and open your eyes wide. Also, open your mouth wide and stick out your tongue, bringing its tip down towards your chin. Pull back your scalp, ears and forehead.
- ꙮ Keeping your face wide open, exhale through your mouth while you contract the muscles at the front of your throat and making a soft and long "haaaaaaaa" sound.

06. *Fire breath*

This breathing technique activates your energy levels. Breathing is done rapidly, rhythmically and continuously. The inhale and the exhale are equal with no pause in between (approximately 2-3 breaths per second). It's always practised through the nostrils with the mouth closed. The fire breath is powered by contractions of the solar plexus, the space just above your belly button. The chest stays relaxed and slightly lifted throughout the breathing cycle.

- ᴥ Exhale through the nose by pulling the belly button inwards and upwards towards the spine. The upper abdominal muscles also pull inwards and upwards.

- ᴥ Inhale by relaxing your abdomen completely and allowing air to be sucked in. Breathing in will happen as part of the relaxation process rather than through any effort of your own.

WARNING: The fire breath can cause light-headedness or make you hyperventilate. If you experience dizziness or faintness when you practise it, stop immediately. If you have lung problems, you should avoid the fire breath as it can make your problem worse.

07. *Chaotic breathing*

This breathing technique energises you and helps you release emotional blockages.

- ᴥ Breathe in and out through your nose as fast and deep as possible.

- ᴥ Repeat this in a non-rhythmic and chaotic pattern for a maximum of 10 minutes.

- ᴥ You can also do this while you're blindfolded so that your focus is on your breathing only.

WARNING: Chaotic breathing can cause light-headedness or make you hyperventilate. If you experience dizziness or faintness when you practise it, stop immediately. If you have lung problems, you should avoid chaotic breathing as it can make your problem worse.

Scanning the body

Consciously scanning our body helps us to become aware of different sensations in our body rather than take them for granted. Focusing our attention on specific parts of our body improves our awareness of our body as a whole. The following is a simple exercise that you can practise.

08. *Body scan*

- 🕉 Find a comfortable place and sit or lie down.

- 🕉 Rest your arms beside you or on your lap.

- 🕉 Close your eyes or look at a fixed point on the floor.

- 🕉 Notice the first few breaths. Notice what the breath feels like as you inhale and exhale. Notice which parts of your nose, mouth, throat and lungs it comes into contact with.

- 🕉 After a few breaths, bring your attention to your feet. Notice any sensations in them. Notice their volume from the inside. Try to feel the skin, the muscles, the tendons, the ligaments and the bones.

- 🕉 Repeat the previous step while moving up your body: ankles, lower legs, knees, thighs, genitals and groin, bum, lower back, belly, chest, upper back, shoulders, upper arms, elbows, forearms, wrists, hands, neck, head and face.

- 🕉 Finally, take a few more breaths and notice how your breath flows through your body as a whole.

Aware movement

Move your hand behind you, outside your field of vision. Now, focus your eyes on a spot in front of you. Without looking at your hand, use it to point at the spot you're looking at. Leaving your hand where it is, glance back at it. Is it pointing towards the spot you were looking at? Yes, it is! This is because our body has receptors that monitor our position in the space around us. Whether we're walking, sitting, standing or running, our body is constantly monitoring our movement even though we're not consciously aware of it.

By increasing our awareness of our movement as it's happening, we can connect to our body more deeply and be more present in it. To do this, it helps to slow down our movement and be aware of the minute sensations that are involved. The following are some exercises that can help you practise aware movement.

09. *Hourly check on posture*

- Set a timer for every hour.
- When the alarm goes off, bring your attention to your posture. Notice how you're holding yourself.
- Check how you can adjust your posture slightly to make it more comfortable.

10. *Walking with awareness*

- Slow down your walking. As you take your next step, notice how the sole of your foot pushes into the ground and how the ground pushes it back.
- Notice how you balance as you lift the other leg. Notice what it feels like to move your leg in space until it reaches the ground in front of you and the sensation of your foot as it pushes into the ground.
- Continue walking like this for a while.
- Finally, stand still for some time and take note of your sensations.
- You can repeat this exercise with any kind of movement.

11. *Dancing with awareness*

- Put on some music. The first few times you try this exercise, it might be more helpful to use music with a slower rhythm.
- Close your eyes. Start feeling the music and allow your body to slowly move freely with it. The aim is to move freely, not to dance in a particular way.
- Notice how your body feels when it's moving. Notice how every movement you make creates a different sensation in the rest of your body. Pay particular attention to how your hip and shoulder movements influence movement in the rest of your body.
- Finally, pause for a while and notice the sensations in your body.

Vocalising

As children, we were often told not to be so noisy, not to cry or not to make a fuss. We were taught to control ourselves and restrain our verbal expression. As a result, this demand to control ourselves might have got stored in our throat leading to a blockage in emotional expression. This might have led us to 'lose our voice' in front of others and not speaking up for ourselves.

Opening up the throat to allow freer emotional expression is a subtle process that can be accompanied by a strong outpouring of emotions. The following are a few exercises that can help you open up the throat area and reclaim your voice.

12.   *Breathing from the back of my throat*

When we breathe, we often use the upper part of our throat. On the other hand, when we exhale, we relax the throat muscles and the windpipe narrows a bit. This exercise uses the lower back of the throat and opens up the windpipe throughout the whole breathing cycle. Use this exercise every time you feel emotionally tense, always checking in with the tension in your throat and widening the windpipe.

- Find a relaxed position.
- Focus on your throat structure. Notice and sense the muscles that hold your throat together, the ones that keep the airway open.
- Bring your attention to how the throat muscles change with every inhale and exhale. Be aware of the sensations in your throat in the same way you would be aware of the movement in your arms when you flex and relax them.
- With the next few inhales, relax the lower back part of your throat. Let the air flow through your nose or mouth and reach the very back of your throat, relaxing it as you do so. You will notice that the sound of your breathing changes and becomes similar to the sound you hear at a cave entrance.
- Focus now on your exhale and try to keep your throat as open as possible. Tense the throat muscles to keep the windpipe wide open while exhaling. You will again notice that you're making a similar sound to when you were inhaling.

- Now, combine the two steps above and keep the airway open during both the inhale and exhale for a few breaths.
- In the end, notice the sensations in your throat.

13.　*Exhaling with sound*

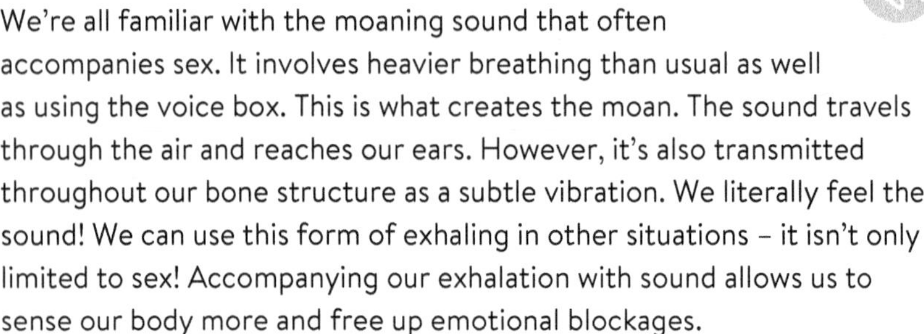

We're all familiar with the moaning sound that often accompanies sex. It involves heavier breathing than usual as well as using the voice box. This is what creates the moan. The sound travels through the air and reaches our ears. However, it's also transmitted throughout our bone structure as a subtle vibration. We literally feel the sound! We can use this form of exhaling in other situations – it isn't only limited to sex! Accompanying our exhalation with sound allows us to sense our body more and free up emotional blockages.

- Find a place where you won't be disturbed.
- Start breathing normally, focusing on the sensation of the breath in your throat.
- Keep the mouth relaxed. Your lips will be partially parted, like when you sigh.
- Exhale through the mouth and, while doing so, start to progressively engage your vocal cords, making a humming sound.
- Explore how tilting your head at different angles influences how easy it is to produce that hum. Find the one that's easiest for you.
- Allow the humming to increase in volume. Breathe from the lower back part of your throat. Notice the vibrations in your throat and possibly other parts of the body.
- Continue exhaling while making sounds and engaging the deepest part of your windpipe as much as possible. You might find that you're also using the top part of your lungs to do so. The aim is not to shout or force air out but to give as much voice as possible to the air as it leaves your throat.

14.　*Breathing out forcefully*

This exercise is about forcing air out of your lungs while giving it a voice. It's about giving yourself power. It's particularly useful if you tend to be withdrawn and not so confident.

- Find a place where you can make noise without restraining yourself, like a remote field, your car or next to a very busy road.

- Take a few breaths while drawing energy from the bottom of your belly, imagining that the energy is coming from your groin.

- Ensure that your throat is as open as possible and that you're breathing from the lower back part of your throat.

- Exhale forcefully in one go, adding sound to it (e.g. "Ahh!"). Increase the volume as much as you can. After each forced exhale, allow yourself to breathe normally a few times and then repeat. You can, of course, shout or scream, but always ensure that the energy is coming from the lower part of your torso through an open windpipe.

- In the end, notice the sensations in your body and what emotions came up in the process.

Touch

Our skin is covered with thousands of sensors that register different forms of touch. The sense of touch is essential for our emotional and psychological development. In fact, people who are deprived of touch when they're young can experience very serious mental health difficulties later on in life.

Touching can be done in diverse ways and we can experience the same kind of touch in different ways depending on the context. For example, if we're feeling irritated and someone caresses our skin, we'll probably feel annoyed even though the same touch from a lover would be arousing. Pain and pleasure can easily be mixed up depending on the situation, as diverse erotic contact teaches us – an arousing tickle for one is annoying for another!

Because it's so important, touch is also a main way in which we can connect to, and feel, our body rather than forget about it. The following are a few exercises to help improve your physical connection to your body.

15. *Touching an object*

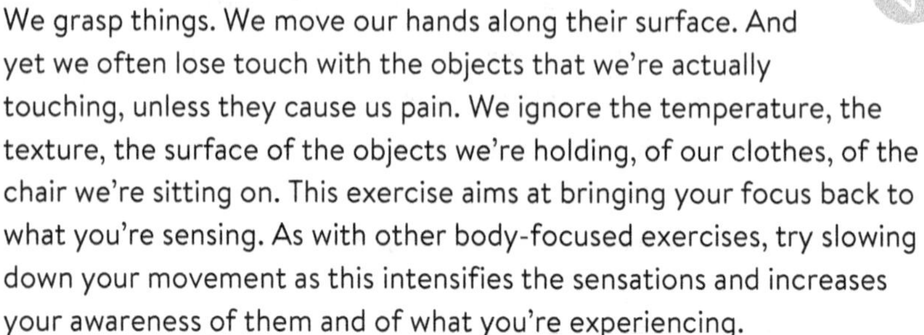

We grasp things. We move our hands along their surface. And yet we often lose touch with the objects that we're actually touching, unless they cause us pain. We ignore the temperature, the texture, the surface of the objects we're holding, of our clothes, of the chair we're sitting on. This exercise aims at bringing your focus back to what you're sensing. As with other body-focused exercises, try slowing down your movement as this intensifies the sensations and increases your awareness of them and of what you're experiencing.

- Find a cushion and place it on your lap.
- Close your eyes and place your hand on the cushion.
- Gently move one of your fingers along the cushion very, very slowly. Notice its texture, its softness, its temperature. Feel its surface dragging along your skin.
- Increase or decrease the pressure of your touch and notice how the sensation changes. Try going faster or slower and, again, notice any changes in sensation.
- Explore it with other fingers. Use the palm and the back of your hand. Notice how different parts of your hand sense the cushion in a different way.
- You can also touch the cushion with your forearm and elbow, always moving slowly and noticing the same things.
- Finally, put both of your hands on your lap and, keeping your eyes closed, notice the sensations in the hand that you used to touch the cushion. Notice how it feels different to the other hand. You might notice that it feels a bit larger.
- You can repeat this exercise with different objects that have different textures, for example, a crumpled piece of paper, a stress ball or a hairbrush.

16. *Touching myself*

When we touch ourselves, we experience touch from two sources: from the part of our body that's touching and from the part of our body that's being touched. By slowing down and focusing on our sense of touch, we can distinguish between the two and heighten the sensation. We also bring more awareness to our body. Maybe we can allow ourselves to venture to parts of our body that we don't usually touch or to use different ways of touching that we've learnt to avoid.

- Find a place where you won't be disturbed.

- Decide which part of your body you would like to explore and remove as much clothing as you feel comfortable with from that part of your body.

- Take some time to move your hands along that part of your body. Move your hands very slowly. Notice the sensation in your hand and the sensation in that part of your body. How does the temperature feel? What about the texture of your skin, its softness? See if there's any part that feels more pleasurable than others.

- Try to see if you can use different parts of your body to touch that same part of your body. Notice how it feels different to when you touched it using your hands. Always be aware of the part of your body that's touching and the part that's being touched.

- Try using different kinds of strokes on that part of your body: a gentle stroke with the fingertips, another softer one with the back of the nails. Try putting more pressure instead. How does it feel to increase the pressure while moving your nails along it, to pinch it softly or harder? What happens when you tap it lightly or harder? Which kind of stroke feels more pleasant for you?

- Finally, lie still and notice the sensations in the part of your body that you were exploring. What did you learn about it?

17. *Holding different parts of my body*

The skin holds us together, literally. By stimulating the sense of pressure in our skin, we can amplify the feeling of being held. This pressure heightens our awareness of the protective layer that lies between us and what's around us. When we feel overwhelmed or exposed, it can help to physically feel the boundary between ourselves and our surroundings.

- Sit comfortably on the floor or on a mat or mattress.
- Keep your eyes closed during the exercise.

- Take a few moments to connect to your breathing and be present in the place you're in at the moment.

- Using both of your hands, hold the tip of one of your feet. Increase the pressure to the point just before it starts feeling uncomfortable. Breathe into this sense of being held and notice how it feels to have that mass of your body in between your hands and to have that part of your body held tight.

- Move your hands to your heel and repeat the previous step. Repeat this process for all parts of your body. There's no need to rush. Just be present with every part you hold. If you don't have time to hold all parts of your body, focus only on some of them. It's better to be present only with some parts of your body than rushing through the exercise trying to touch the whole of your body. Remember to include your genitals and other erotic zones in the process.

- Finally, lie still for a while and take note of the sensations on your skin.

OUR MIND AND EMOTIONS

Another two fundamental aspects of ourselves are our mind and our emotions, intrinsically linked to our body. We will now take a closer look at them.

OUR EMOTIONS

Emotions are automatic responses that help us deal with events without first having to think about them. If something explodes next to me, I feel afraid. If I eat a delicious meal, I feel happy. If someone I love dies, I feel sad. Emotions inform us how to act.

Emotions happen, and so we cannot control whether or not we feel them. What we can control is how we behave after we feel them. If I feel afraid, I can decide to run away or to stay where I am. If I feel angry, I can decide to become physically violent or to keep calm and behave respectfully.

Because emotions are automatic responses, they can end up being outside of our awareness. If we're caught up in what we're doing or thinking, we can lose touch with what we're feeling. We might have gone through a painful life experience and so learnt to shut down our emotions so as not to feel the pain. However, this doesn't mean that they do not affect us. Instead, they end up influencing our life without us being aware of them. Like a puppeteer, they pull the strings that make us act in particular ways. For example, if, as a child, I was afraid of one of my parents because they shouted at me a lot, as an adult I might be inclined to choose jobs where I don't need to interact with people in authority. My fear is unconsciously making me avoid situations where someone might shout at me again. This doesn't mean that this is necessarily what will happen. The opposite might be true or I might have become a very unpleasant person myself! But emotions that are outside of our awareness will always tend to impact our behaviour.

In order to live a fuller life, it's vital that we connect to our emotions. By bringing them into the foreground, they won't continue impacting our life without us realising. Being aware of them also allows us to integrate them into our lives and use them to our advantage rather than wasting a lot of energy trying to block them out.

Throughout this book, you will often be asked to check what you're feeling. This isn't an easy process for everyone as, at times, we lack the words to describe what we're feeling. To facilitate this process, below you will find a series of lists of emotions. Each list consists of a number of emotions that can be grouped together. The words in each group reflect different facets or levels of intensity of the same kind of emotion. The first few lists refer to more pleasant emotions, while the rest refer to more unpleasant ones.

Calmness

- Calm
- Serene
- Peaceful
- Relaxed
- Relieved
- Liberated

Empathy

- Empathetic
- Compassionate

Excitement

᪰ Curious	᪰ Captivated
᪰ Inquisitive	᪰ Aroused
᪰ Intrigued	᪰ Bewitched
᪰ Eager	᪰ Amused
᪰ Enthused	᪰ Excited
᪰ Interested	᪰ Thrilled

Happiness

᪰ Content	᪰ Ecstatic
᪰ Pleased	᪰ Elated
᪰ Cheerful	᪰ Exhilarated
᪰ Glad	᪰ Euphoric
᪰ Delighted	᪰ Grateful
᪰ Happy	᪰ Satisfied
᪰ Joyful	᪰ Proud
᪰ Blissful	᪰ Invigorated
᪰ Jubilant	᪰ Energetic

Hope

᪰ Confident	᪰ Inspired
᪰ Optimistic	᪰ Hopeful
᪰ Encouraged	᪰ Motivated

Love and Sexual desire

᪰ Affectionate	᪰ Lustful
᪰ Infatuated	᪰ Horny
᪰ Sensual	᪰ Passionate

Surprise

᪰ Startled	᪰ Astounded
᪰ Astonished	᪰ Shocked
᪰ Surprised	᪰ Dumbstruck
᪰ Amazed	᪰ Awestruck

Anger

- Irritated
- Grumpy
- Annoyed
- Frustrated
- Aggravated
- Indignant
- Angry
- Exasperated
- Enraged
- Furious
- Infuriated
- Mad
- Outraged
- Spiteful
- Critical
- Sceptical
- Aggressive
- Vengeful

Anxiety

- Uneasy
- Perturbed
- Agitated
- Nervous
- Apprehensive
- Concerned
- Worried
- Anxious

Confusion

- Unfocused
- Uncertain
- Dazed
- Puzzled
- Perplexed
- Confused
- Disoriented
- Disconcerted
- Bewildered
- Overwhelmed

Disconnection

- Distant
- Disconnected
- Detached
- Indifferent
- Bored
- Apathetic
- Numb
- Isolated
- Alienated
- Lonely
- Excluded
- Abandoned
- Rejected
- Betrayed

Disgust

- Averse
- Contemptuous
- Disgusted
- Nauseated
- Revolted
- Loathsome
- Repulsed
- Hateful
- Horrified
- Appalled

Fear

- Insecure
- Exposed
- Alarmed
- Panicked
- Threatened
- Afraid
- Scared
- Terrified

Hopelessness

- Dissatisfied
- Displeased
- Disappointed
- Disillusioned
- Discouraged
- Pessimistic
- Dispirited
- Disheartened
- Demoralised
- Despairing
- Helpless
- Out of control
- Powerless
- Hopeless

Jealousy

- Envious
- Jealous
- Resentful
- Bitter

Sadness

- Troubled
- Gloomy
- Melancholic
- Low-spirited
- Distressed
- Despondent
- Unhappy
- Sad
- Depressed
- Miserable
- Sorrowful
- Grief-stricken

Shame and Guilt

- Guilty
- Contrite
- Regretful
- Remorseful
- Mortified
- Shy

- Awkward
- Embarrassed
- Humiliated
- Fragile
- Vulnerable
- Ashamed

Suffering

- Stressed
- Hurt

- Anguished
- Agonised

If you struggle to get in touch with your emotions or find that you're often not aware of them, find moments during the day when you check in with your emotions. Ask yourself: "What am I feeling right now?" You can use the list above to help you identify specific emotions or you can add others. Try to stick to using a single word to describe what you're feeling, otherwise, you would most probably be expressing what you're thinking instead.

OUR MIND

One of our greatest strengths as human beings is our ability to think in very complex and abstract ways. Our cognitive abilities allow us to understand what's happening around us, make sense of it, see patterns and predict what's likely to happen in the future. If you snap at me when I talk to you and this happens many times, my mind will learn that pattern and expect that, the next time I speak to you, you will act in the same way.

Through this understanding, we also gain a sense of control over our environment. We reduce the amount of unknown we're surrounded by. For example, thinking about how much money we usually spend allows us to budget, which in turn reduces the risk of depleting our financial resources. Understanding also allows us to plan for emergencies and create order in chaotic situations, like someone being seriously injured.

Our thinking also enables us to generate purpose in life, which in turn motivates us for action. For example, believing that we should live in a just society can lead us to donate money to organisations that help those with fewer resources. And wanting to travel for a year can motivate us to do various odd jobs in order to save enough money for the trip.

Thinking is intimately related to other aspects of ourselves, like our emotions and our body language. Our thoughts can directly affect our emotions. If we see someone with a frown on their face, we might initially think that they don't like us. As a result, we also start thinking that they're an unfriendly person and we start distancing ourselves from them. But when they tell us that they had a very strong headache, we change our understanding of their frown. Consequently, our emotions towards that person change. We try to see how we can help them ease their headache. Instead of irritation, we experience care towards them.

Although we possess high cognitive abilities, these aren't perfect as they aren't objective. All our thinking takes place in our brain and so our mind becomes both judge and jury! To top it all, in order to facilitate the processing of information, our mind takes a lot of shortcuts. As a result, we generate automatic thinking patterns to make it easier to judge similar situations. However, these patterns can easily be distorted ones and, given that they're automatic, it's difficult for us to notice them. The following is a list of different kinds of thinking errors that we can make. Most of them can apply to both negative and positive things.

Thinking error	Description and example
Absolute statements	Thinking in terms of 'always' or 'never'. *e.g. Thinking that you should always look your best, otherwise people won't like you.*
All-or-nothing thinking	Looking at things in an absolute way. Either everything is entirely good or everything is entirely bad. *e.g. Thinking that, unless you get everything completely right, you're a failure.*

Always being right	Believing that your beliefs, thoughts, emotions and actions are always right. This can include using other sources to legitimise your position, such as status or gender.
Catastrophising	Assuming that the worst will always happen in a situation you find difficult. *e.g. Assuming that, if someone you love is going to ride a motorbike, they will almost certainly be involved in an accident.*
Denying (and blaming)	Never accepting your own responsibility in a situation. *e.g. Having regular arguments with your partner and believing that they're the only cause of the arguments because, for example, they're very uptight.*
Double standards	Judging your behaviour and that of others using two different measures. *e.g. Believing that it's OK that your partner forgets to do the shopping, but being very critical of yourself for having forgotten, or vice versa.*
Emotional reasoning	Deciding only on the basis of your emotions. *e.g. Feeling angry at someone and reacting disrespectfully because that's 'what you felt'.* *e.g. Immediately trusting a stranger with very personal information just because 'it felt right'.*
Fortune-telling	Believing that you can predict the future from some past events. *e.g. After having had a couple of dates and being dumped, you conclude that you will always be dumped if you go for other dates.*

Labelling	Identifying yourself or others with a shortcoming and not separating the person from the action. *e.g. Making a mistake and instead of saying "I made a mistake", thinking, "I'm a fool!" Or thinking this in relation to someone else who makes a mistake.*
Magnification	Blowing things out of proportion. *e.g. Thinking that, because of a spelling mistake you made in an email, you risk losing your job. e.g. Thinking that, because of a small achievement at work, you're the best employee in the company.*
Mental filtering	Picking out a negative detail and dwelling on it regardless of other positives. *e.g. A driver shouts insults at you while you're on your way to work in the morning and you continue dwelling on it all day long.*
Mind-reading	Assuming that people react negatively (or positively) to you even though there's no evidence for it. *e.g. Assuming that a colleague at work doesn't like you just because, in the first week of your employment, they haven't as yet said hello to you. e.g. Assuming that everybody likes you even though you may actually be actively irritating others.*
Minimisation	Downplaying successes and making them less significant than they would be for others. *e.g. Receiving a top award and thinking that it doesn't actually reflect any ability on your side.*

Overgeneralisation	Treating one negative event as a general rule of how bad things are.
	e.g. You have a bad experience with a bus driver and conclude that all bus drivers are rude and that it's better to avoid using buses.
Personalising	Making situations 'about you' even though they may not necessarily be so.
	e.g. Thinking that you're unlovable because your boyfriend or girlfriend had sex with someone else.
'Should' statements	Criticising yourself, others or situations with 'should' or 'ought to' statements.
	e.g. Thinking that others should find my jokes funny. *e.g. Thinking that if I put in a lot of work, I should always be rewarded for it.*

So as not to allow these automatic thinking patterns to dictate our behaviours, it's important to develop our awareness of them. It helps to adopt a 'third-person approach' to understand them better and instead start interpreting things differently. This book includes a lot of exercises aimed at helping you develop insight into your thinking patterns. However, the following are some exercises to help you increase your overall awareness of them.

01. *Journaling*

Journaling isn't just about writing down what you ate and whom you met every day. It's about taking some time every day or two, or after particularly emotional moments, to write down what happened inside you. Note down the situation, your thoughts, emotions and body sensations. Write about what your anticipation of the future is and what you learnt about yourself from the situation. When journaling, you're not writing a book. Focus on expressing your thoughts rather than using perfect grammar and punctuation. You might want to revisit those pages at a later date or you might just want to get your experience down on a page and move on.

02. *An unending stream of writing*

This exercise is very similar to journaling. However, in this case, give yourself 5 to 10 minutes, preferably every day in the morning, and start writing continuously. Ignore any sentence structure. Just focus on immediately capturing what's going through your mind. If you aren't noticing anything, you can write something like "I'm not noticing anything" or anything else that you're thinking. Don't stop until the time is over.

03. *Creative expression*

Words are great ways of expressing oneself. However, our rational side can prevent us from freely expressing ourselves. Trauma can block our memories. Moral beliefs can inhibit our desires. By using a creative medium, we can capture other thoughts that we have before they're censured by our rational mind. There's no limit to creative expression. Draw, play around with clay or sand, create a piece of music, dance. The important thing here is not to focus on the final result but on the actual expression and what sense you make out of it.

04. *Examining the cognitive distortions*

Start noticing which cognitive distortions you use in different situations. How are you interpreting your colleague's tone of voice? And how did you react when the tickets you wanted were sold out just before you decided to buy them? When investigating our cognitive distortions, it's also helpful to explore what underlying beliefs we may have about life. For example, if we have a list of 'should' and 'must' statements to follow, we might actually have an inner belief that we're only lovable if we're good. If we're constantly catastrophising outcomes, we might have the belief that we aren't safe. Use the following table to help you note down and explore your cognitive distortions and the underlying beliefs.

Situation	Thoughts	Thinking error	Underlying belief
e.g. One of my colleagues told me that I needed to improve something.	*e.g. I'm really incompetent in my work and also in my life in general.*	*e.g. Over-generalisation.*	*e.g. I'm not a competent person.*
e.g. One of my colleagues told me that I needed to improve something.	*e.g. I'm really incompetent in my work and also in my life in general.*	*e.g. Over-generalisation.*	*e.g. I'm not a competent person.*

04

OTHER ASPECTS OF OURSELVES

We will now briefly touch upon other important aspects of ourselves, namely our behaviour, our past and our relationship with the world around us. Finally, we will make a brief reference to the experience of what lies beyond the self.

OUR BEHAVIOUR

Our emotions and thoughts impact how we act. However, the opposite can also be true. If we change our behaviour, we can start changing how we feel and think.

Think about your facial expression when you're feeling confused, angry, displeased, sad or worried. You probably end up frowning. On the other hand, if you're feeling happy, content and serene, you end up smiling. What would happen if you change your facial expression regardless of what you're feeling? What would happen if you start frowning even though you don't have any negative feelings? You may start feeling some negativity because the more you frown, the more you will be disposed to feel negative. On the other hand, if you decide to smile when you're not particularly happy, you may notice that your mood will lighten up. This is because our muscles feed back information to our brain, informing it of how we're feeling. So, we can use our body to 'trick' our mind into believing we're feeling differently from how we actually are.

This also applies to our beliefs. If we believe we feel uncomfortable being around people, we tend to avoid social contact. Changing this behaviour and instead deciding to be around people, while telling ourselves that it's OK to do so, will, in the long run, make it easier to be around others.

When we're not feeling great about something, we tend to dwell on it and it becomes a 'comfortable' space because it's what we know. Taking action and changing our behaviour is challenging, but it can be the easiest way to bring about change. So, sometimes, all we need to do is to act regardless of how we feel or what we think!

OUR PAST

If one observes a pair of identical twins, one can always tell them apart. Although they're genetically the same, their bodies have changed in a unique way. Our body is always impacted by our life experience. Age changes our body. Accidents and wounds leave a physical trace on our body. This impact of life experience doesn't only apply to our body. It also affects our way of thinking, feeling and relating to others. And the younger we are when the experience happens, the stronger its impact is likely to be.

As children, we don't have a lot of experience behind us. This limits the way we understand situations and we can easily end up generalising. As a result of this, what we experience as kids can often lay the foundation for how we perceive reality later on in life. For example, if we grow up in a caring environment, we learn that people are safe and trustworthy. On the other hand, if we grow up in an environment surrounded by adults who treated us badly for no apparent reason, we conclude that we aren't safe around people. Similarly, if we were neglected while growing up, we might learn that we can only rely on ourselves because no one will provide for us. These conclusions tend to become general frameworks that determine how we live out future experiences and relationships.

Some people continue developing in line with their childhood life experiences and, as adults, live out similar patterns. However, others rebel against these experiences and, as adults, live very differently from how they were as kids. Someone who was neglected as a child might turn out to be a very generous and trusting adult. Or someone who came from a house plagued by domestic violence can turn out to be a very peaceful person. This is because we're able to learn from all of our life experiences. A caring aunt or uncle, a good friend at school or a loving partner can all help us reshape the initial perception of reality that we had as kids. Therefore, regardless of our upbringing, as long as we're open to learning from new experiences, we're not condemned to a specific way of being as an adult. Nevertheless, we can never ignore the fact that past experiences have an impact on us.

Throughout this book, we will be looking at our past experiences in relation to specific topics. The reason isn't to get stuck in the past. Instead, by looking at our past, we can understand where we come from and why we behave, think and feel the way we do. We can then integrate the past into our lives and bring about the necessary changes to take our life in a different direction.

The desire for change and the actions we take are driven by our conscious mind but our tendencies are strongly impacted by our past. When we're stressed, we tend to revert to our default ways of behaving. So, when that happens, be gentle with yourself. Use your understanding of your past to recognise why you tend to act, think or feel in that way and, once again, take a step forwards onto the path of growth you want to follow.

THE RELATIONAL DIMENSION

Physics talks a lot about forces between different objects, regardless of their size. Gravity is an example of this. The Earth is constantly pulling us towards it. However, at the same time, we're also pulling it towards us. But given that we're extremely small compared to the size of the Earth, it is us that end up being physically pulled towards the Earth rather than pulling it up with us whenever we decide to jump! The same force of gravity exists between every single object. It exists between you and the book you're reading, between you and the cup of tea or coffee you might be sipping. And it also exists between you and every other person. We're too small in size to feel the pull, but the force between us exists just the same.

There are also other forces at play in nature. Unlike gravity, some of them involve both attraction and repulsion. We all know how two magnets attract each other. And yet, the moment we turn one of them around, they try to push away from each other at all costs! This is because there's a magnetic force between them.

Gravity and magnetism are just two examples of forces that exist between objects – attracting each other or pushing each other away. This is because everything that exists is always in relation to everything else around it. As human beings, we're constantly in a relationship with the Earth, with nature and with our immediate environment.

Being in that relationship also implies that we constantly have an impact on each other. A dark, dull place will affect how we feel and what we do very differently from when we're in a bright, open space. Our behaviour will, in turn, affect the environment we're in. The environmentalist movement is a testimony to how we're never in isolation – we always exist in relation to everything that's around us.

The same applies to us as human beings. We're intrinsically relational beings. Unfortunately, humanity has very often been caught up in its cognitive abilities. This has led us to focus on our identity as individuals, on our ways of thinking, on our value systems and on our own desires. In the process, we often forget that we're never just an individual. We always share a relationship with others, even from before we're born! How others are present or absent to us will have an impact on us, and our way of being with others will have an impact on them. We're never outside of this relational space because, even when we're alone, we're actually experiencing that space as a lack of something we need.

This has a particular significance in romantic relationships. Here it's not just about what I do and what my partner does. Instead, the relationship dynamic acquires a life of its own. A strong example of this is when sex is experienced as something that transcends oneself. In this way, it becomes an experience of the relational space between those involved.

The relational and sexual dimensions are too important and complex to try to squeeze them into a few pages of this book. They merit a space entirely for themselves. Hence, in this book, we will primarily be focusing on our individual experiences. However, it's important to remember that this is only part of the story. Who we were in our past, who we are in the present and who we will become in the future is always lived out in a relational context.

BEYOND THE SELF

Evolution has provided human beings with a very complex brain. This has given us powerful cognitive tools that enable us to be creative. It makes it possible for us to think about, and imagine, the future. But being able to think about what might happen means that we can also think about what might *not* happen. In other words, because of our ability to imagine the future, our mind is also aware of the possibility of us no longer existing. This thought can trigger the stress response that we will be talking about in the next chapter. It generates worry and anxiety about the future and can lead to existential anxiety: the sense of anxiety about our existence and survival. After all, the more we think about it, the more we realise that it's a really big feat to manage to stay alive!

Denying existential anxiety

Some of us flee this existential anxiety by denying it. We do this by thinking of ourselves as especially important creatures. Everything becomes about ourselves. We become the pinnacle of creation as if the aim of the whole universe was to finally produce human beings! It leads us to believe that we have the right to survive at all costs, regardless of the impact on the environment and other people. It makes us think that we can manipulate divine powers to provide us with what we want or that the universe is intently trying to understand our individual needs and provide accordingly. But, in doing so, we disconnect from our scary reality, from acknowledging that we're ultimately insignificant in the face of Nature. Our existence as human beings is an unimaginably small fraction of time in comparison to the duration of the universe. When the human species dies out, the universe will continue being as it always was – without us. However, being constantly aware of this can generate existential anxiety which we try our best to shield ourselves from and, in doing so, we set ourselves up for other problems!

This false sense of importance that we have as human beings lies at the root of many social, political and psychological problems. Our sense of importance and entitlement can make us crave power, lead us to harm others and the environment, and give us a false expectation of how life should be for us. When our hopes and desires aren't fulfilled or when things don't turn out as we wanted them to, we can end up feeling anxious or sad. But, in this case, these feelings can be the result of our unfulfilled expectations that stem from that sense of self-importance.

Being humble

Another way we can deal with this type of existential crisis is to acknowledge our vulnerability and insignificance by exercising humbleness. The word 'humble' is a word that comes from the Latin word 'humus', which means 'ground'. Being humble is about accepting our insignificance and acknowledging that we aren't greater than the earth we walk upon.

The aim of humbleness, however, isn't to be stuck in a downward spiral of self-pity or low self-esteem. On the contrary, it's about recognising where we stand while acknowledging that which is greater and vaster than we are. People from different walks of life and diverse cultures have referred to this in various ways, including: Energy, Life force, God, Universe, Qi, the Spiritual and Nature.

Facing that which is greater than us is an experience involving a mix of wonder and terror. We experience it when we stand in front of a mountain, when we're out on a boat in a vast expanse of sea with no land in sight or when we look up at the night sky. We experience it in moments of sexual ecstasy and in our creative endeavours. But we also experience it in the form of natural disasters, such as earthquakes, floods and fires. In all of these situations and many others, we become aware that we're facing something greater than we are and that acts regardless of us.

It would be beyond the scope of this book to explore this aspect further. However, as you work through this book, you're invited to explore where and how you situate yourself in relation to that which is greater and the importance you allocate to yourself and your expectations. Although this can be a psychologically and emotionally challenging process, it allows us to assess our desires and expectations in order to align ourselves with the present moment.

❧ 05 ❧

OUR RESPONSE TO STRESS

Bring to mind a test you sat for, a new project you're about to launch, a job interview or perhaps someone yelling at you. All of these situations cause stress. They make us feel emotionally upset and physically tense. They might make us feel worried or anxious. But we usually overcome the situation and move on with our life.

However, some events can be deeply distressing. We can experience these events directly, like if we were to be assaulted, for example. We can also witness them happening to others, like if we were to witness a car accident. Or we can just get to know about them, like when we hear about something horrible on the news. It's also possible that these events aren't an actual threat but only one we're perceiving. In the face of such events, we feel unable to cope and we react emotionally, mentally and physically. We feel helpless, shocked and overwhelmed. We feel dizzy and shaky. Our muscles tense up or we faint. We lose our concentration and blank out. This reaction is different to the one we experience in the face of the usual stress. It has a stronger impact on us. We have experienced trauma.

The nervous system

Before understanding trauma in some more detail, let us look at what happens in our body when we normally experience stress.

Our nervous system is constantly at work. Our senses perceive what's happening in our environment and our brain processes all of that information. It decides what to store, what to ignore and whether we need to take any action.

The brain is made up of different areas. One of these areas, called the *amygdala*, deals with managing emotional responses. It's a small structure, the size of an almond, lying deep in the centre of our brain. Another area is the *hippocampus*: a finger-like structure, the size of a headphone jack, attached to the amygdala. One of the functions of the hippocampus is to store experiences in long-term memory. The other area we will consider here is the large outer part of the brain, called the *cortex*, which is also involved in the storage of memories.

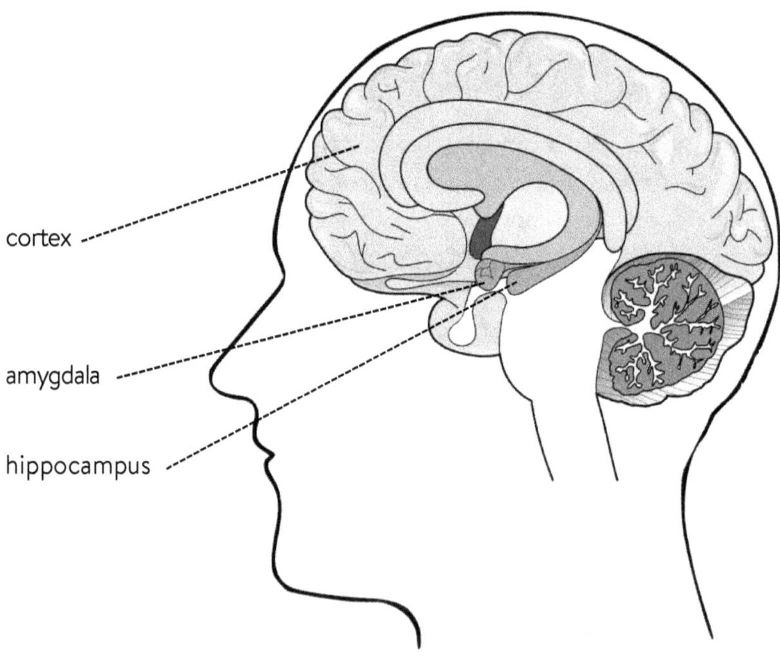

The brain regulates how the body functions using two different nerve networks. The *sympathetic nervous system* prepares the body for immediate action. It increases blood supply to important organs, readies us for sudden movement and focuses our senses, thus making us more aware of our environment. When this system is activated, we experience most, or all, of the following:

- Faster and stronger heartbeat
- Increase in blood pressure
- Rapid breathing
- Dry mouth
- Sweating
- Increase in muscle tension
- Widening of the pupils
- Relaxation of the bladder

The other system is called the *parasympathetic nervous system*. It's responsible for making us feel relaxed and is the system that's active when we're asleep. It works in the opposite way to the sympathetic nervous system. When it's activated, we experience most, or all, of the following:

- Slower heartbeat
- Decrease in blood pressure
- Slower and shallower breathing
- Salivation in the mouth
- Decrease in muscle tension and going limp
- Narrowing of the pupils
- Constriction of the bladder

Our reaction to threat

We can experience a sense of threat in two ways. The first involves an actual threat. This is when there's a real danger of something happening to us, physically or emotionally, like if we're mugged in the street, a dog growls at us, we're humiliated in front of our peers or we're betrayed by our partner.

The second way involves a perceived threat. In this case, we interpret an event as being potentially dangerous and we react to it as if the danger were real. We hear fireworks going off in the distance but react as if they're exploding right next to us. Or we receive a meeting request from our boss and we start shaking and sweating as we picture ourselves getting fired.

Despite our ability to process highly complex information, our brain doesn't immediately distinguish between an actual and a perceived threat. That's why we automatically pull our head back when a dinosaur lunges at us in a 3D movie! In that specific moment, our brain perceives it as a real danger.

The reason we automatically pull our head back in the above example is that our stress response has been activated. This means that the information arriving from the senses – our eyes, in this case – has been assessed by the amygdala as indicating a threat and the amygdala informs other parts of the brain to act accordingly. This process triggers the stress response in our brain, often referred to as the *fight-or-flight response*.

Flight

If we believe that we can survive the threat, the sympathetic nervous system is activated. This prepares us to either fight or flee. If our mind concludes that we can flee, it prepares our body for immediate escape. For example, if we're faced with a group of attackers, we can find ourselves running away faster than we're usually able to run. The same flight response can be activated even in situations that rationally don't call for physically running away from something. We might be sitting for an important exam or waiting for an appointment with the dentist. Our limbs become restless. We become fidgety and tense. Our eyes constantly dart around and we feel trapped. We want to run away.

Fight

On the other hand, our mind can conclude that we can overpower what's threatening us or that we're trapped so we can only fight back. In this case, the fight mode is activated. For example, after we ran away from our attackers we ended up in a dead-end and they're blocking the exit. So, we brace ourselves to fight them off. Our jaws tighten, our arms tense up, our stomach feels knotted and we feel like punching or kicking them. However, we can also go into fight mode even if we're not being physically attacked. A colleague at work might have made fun of us in front of others or someone damaged our car during the night. In these cases, we can still experience the sensations of being in fight mode and can, at times, end up behaving in a way that impacts us negatively.

Freeze

There are also, however, situations where we cannot flee from the threat or fight it off. When this happens, our brain focuses on how we can survive until we're able to fight or flee. It activates the parasympathetic nervous system and we go into shutdown mode. Different parts of the brain are switched off, especially those concerned with speaking and reasoning. Our body slows down, our limbs go limp and our body posture collapses. Our eyes space out, our skin grows pale and we feel numb. We might throw up or lose control of our bladder or bowels. We can even end up fainting. Due to the endorphins being released in our blood, we feel less pain. We dissociate from our feelings so that we don't experience terror. This total shutdown protects us from both physical and emotional pain with the hope that, at some point, it will be possible to switch back into fight-or-flight mode. For example, if our attackers overpower us, we feel helpless and freeze. We disconnect from our body. We might also not be able to remember what happened during the attack. The same might happen if we have to sing on a stage, if we're humiliated by our boss in front of our colleagues or if we experience sexual abuse.

As a result of having activated the freeze response, our mind can remain stuck in that experience. Even after the danger is well past, the brain continues constantly waiting for a moment to go into fight or flight mode. This can lead to rage outbursts, anxiety, depression, sleep disturbances and many other mental health difficulties. In these cases, we end up stuck in our incomplete response to the initial threat. We get locked in trauma.

Different aspects of trauma

We can observe what we've just described above also happening in animals when they're hunted down. They run away, fight off the predator or just go limp when captured and then suddenly spring back to life the moment there's a chance of escape. Likewise, if we're attacked by someone, involved in an accident or are sexually abused, our physical safety is threatened and so our stress response kicks in. However, this response is also activated when we experience emotional or psychological threats, like being shamed in front of peers, scolded by a teacher or constantly criticised by a parent. In these situations, the fight, flight or freeze responses get activated in the same way, as if there's a physical danger.

We often think of trauma in relation to a single big event. However, it can also be the result of an accumulation of smaller events that slowly, but constantly, chip away at our sense of safety. We might be regularly criticised by our caregivers or subtly bullied at school. Because in these situations we feel trapped in an unsafe situation, we experience the same effects as if we had experienced a single, big traumatic event. This accumulation can be such that, for some of us, all of our life becomes a series of minor traumas. As a result, we experience a sense of being stuck as they remain active in our brain and feed into an overall sense of being in danger. Our stress response ends up being always mildly activated, negatively impacting our perception of ourselves and our interaction with others.

Trauma and memory

Trauma also impacts our memories. If the trauma is not resolved, the sense of danger remains constantly on our mind. As a result, the traumatic experience isn't processed so it doesn't move to long-term memory. Instead, it constantly triggers the amygdala which makes us feel like we're reliving the experience in the present moment and, every time, it triggers the stress response.

However, trauma isn't only stored in our brain but also as a body memory. For example, a traumatic event can be stored as tension in our muscles or as limpness. It can be stored as suppression of our defence system against illnesses or as an imbalance in hormones. In turn, this will constantly signal to our brain that we're still in danger and so it maintains the current state of trauma. Until our mind gets over the traumatic experience, our body will remain stuck in that physical state that was triggered by the traumatic experience.

When trauma becomes Post-Traumatic Stress

In some cases, the stress response can linger for a long period of time with very negative consequences. This is called Post-Traumatic Stress Disorder (PTSD). In this case, we experience some of the following symptoms, at times even many years after the traumatic event:

- Flashbacks, that is, re-experiencing the traumatic event as if it's happening now
- Night terrors or nightmares
- Difficulty in going to sleep or regularly waking up early
- Recollections of the traumatic event coming up without any particular trigger
- Avoidance of anything related to the trauma (e.g. we always take a much longer route to avoid passing from where the negative experience happened)
- Anger or rage for no particular reason
- Mood swings without any particular reason
- Depressed mood and decreased interest in life for no particular reason
- Being extremely vigilant and very easily startled
- Finding it hard to concentrate
- Withdrawing from others for no particular reason
- Excessively blaming ourselves
- Having memory blanks concerning the traumatic event

Healing from trauma

Suffering from trauma doesn't mean that we're doomed to carry it around with us throughout our life. It is possible to heal from trauma, although the healing process can, in itself, be quite difficult at times. The following are three main ways that help this healing to happen.

- Practise ways of calming down the stress response and strong emotional reactions. Any kind of body awareness exercise is helpful, such as mindfulness, meditation, yoga or breathing exercises like the ones described in chapter 02 (p. 9).

- Activate the body through exercise, like doing some sports activity or going to the gym. This helps you to discharge pent-up energy and physically go against the freeze response.

- Interact with other people. Find safe places where you feel comfortable and slowly learn to trust again. Support groups can be particularly useful when dealing with specific difficult experiences.

Although the above suggestions can be helpful in healing trauma, they might not be enough. If you feel that you have unresolved or unpleasant emotions or memories surrounding your trauma, it's advisable to speak to a professional therapist who's trained to work with trauma.

SECTION B

THE
WORK

~ 06 ~

ON THINKING AND FEELING

Some of us tend to give more importance to our thoughts, while others prioritise emotions. This shapes how we look at life and interact with others. If we're more pragmatic and logical, we can come across as cold and uncaring. If we're more expressive and empathetic, we can come across as overly emotional and unreliable.

At times, we might find ourselves torn between these two dimensions when our head says one thing but our heart says another. This is because, to a greater or lesser extent, we all have both a thinking side and a feeling side to ourselves. However, at different moments in our lives, we tend to lean more towards one of these dimensions. Let's take a closer look at each one of them.

Audio files for this chapter can be accessed at
thehorsesmouth.michaelconti.net/lbwy-ch06
or by scanning the adjacent QR code.

Being mainly focused on one's thoughts

People who focus mainly on their thoughts base decisions about their behaviours and relationships on what they see as being true. They're rational, they like order and structure and they keep their cool when making decisions under pressure. They're good at problem-solving because they think things through very well. This often means that they evaluate things relentlessly. They're able to sort ideas, find inconsistencies and analyse the pros and cons of a situation.

These are very useful skills to have in various situations. Having such a mindset is crucial when we need to take action without our stress response being fully activated. We want firefighters to enter a burning building and put out the fire, not get all emotional and run away screaming! Being mainly focused on thinking also comes in handy when one has a goal to achieve. By focusing on the practical implications and analysing the planning that's involved for any inconsistencies, there's a higher chance that the plan succeeds and that it's a more effective and efficient one.

However, being primarily focused on thinking also comes with its drawbacks. People who engage primarily with their thoughts are inclined to focus primarily on the task at hand and ignore the relational dimension. An example of this is a manager who only focuses on business outcomes and doesn't consider the relationship with employees. Because they tend to ignore the relational aspect, people who engage mainly with their thinking often come across as blunt, business-like, uncaring and indifferent.

Another difficulty that comes with focusing primarily on thinking is a higher chance of dismissing other people's emotions. This often implies judging the use of emotions in decision-making as a weakness. This can cause problems in romantic relationships or at work, especially if the other person tends to give more importance to the emotional side.

When people who engage mainly with thinking disconnect from their emotions, it doesn't only generate problems with others but also with themselves. This is because, when we ignore our emotions, we discount a crucial motivational centre in our brain. Emotions provide us with invaluable information about what's beneficial for us, or not. So, when we focus mainly on the rational side, we lose out on this information that can further enlighten our decision-making processes.

Although focusing primarily on thinking can lead to discounting emotions, it doesn't mean that emotions aren't present. Instead, it means that emotions are being restrained or suppressed, which results in losing touch with a vital aspect of oneself.

Being mainly focused on emotions

Some people prioritise their emotions. They tend to be more people-centred and value-oriented in their approach to life. They tend to be creative and freely express their emotions. They're often warm, caring, compassionate and empathetic. They can connect very well with others and try to establish and maintain harmony within a group. They bring joy and enthusiasm and are great at motivating others. They can also be very intuitive people. This doesn't mean that they aren't able to use their rational side. It only means that their decisions are shaped primarily by their emotions and the relational dimension of life.

On the downside, people who focus primarily on emotions can, at times, experience their feelings gaining the upper hand. They can be easily impacted by what's happening around them. This can lead them to feel that they're at the mercy of other things happening in their life and that they have no control. As a result, people who engage mainly with their emotions might be more inclined to react to situations rather than being more proactive and take planned action.

Given the power that emotions have, if they're the primary focus in our life, they can lead us to experience a constant level of intensity that can be draining and overwhelming. At times, this emotional energy ends up being channelled into anger that can be unleashed in a very destructive way. An example of this is when people lash out at their partners in relationships, saying or doing things they later regret because they weren't thinking about what was happening. This, then, makes it very difficult to repair the rupture that was caused in the relationship. Because some people who focus mainly on emotions experience difficulty with confrontation and have a strong need for harmony, they can sometimes avoid hard truths and turn a blind eye towards abusive situations. Those who are more engaged with their emotions can also come across as idealistic and indirect, often triggering annoyance in people who are more engaged with their thinking!

Stepping out from the struggle

Having a rational and structured aspect in us that functions well helps us see things more objectively without being necessarily caught up in what's happening. However, it's also important to be informed by our emotions, especially when it comes to the relational side of our life. And given that we're social beings, this means that this aspect is present in most of the situations we're in.

Although thinking and feeling can be perceived as opposites, in reality they aren't. They're two dimensions of ourselves that feed into each other. As described in chapter 03, our thoughts generate our emotions and these, in turn, trigger what we think. By learning how to access both our emotions and our thinking, we can utilise their synergy and avoid being caught up in a battle between the two.

To be able to access and utilise both of these dimensions, it's helpful to make good use of our body as it has the capacity to contain both of them. Focusing on our body provides us with an opportunity to step out of the struggle between our thoughts and our feelings and instead connect with both dimensions. Nurturing the experience of being rooted in our body is vital because, ultimately, our thoughts and emotions are temporary in nature, but our body is permanently present for as long as we live.

How to be more balanced in your thoughts and feelings

The following are some suggestions to help you develop a more balanced approach to your thinking and feeling.

- Identify what emotions you're feeling. Use words to describe them. Make use of the list of emotions found in chapter 03 (p. 22).
- Instead of avoiding your emotions, try to become aware of them and acknowledge them. Ask yourself:
  - What am I feeling?
  - Why am I feeling these emotions?
  - What triggered my emotions in this situation?
  - Is there anything in my past that makes me more prone to feel, or not feel, these emotions?

- ∂ Learn to express your emotions. Find a friend, a family member or a therapist, coach or other professional and make an effort to articulate your emotions. Ask them to help you talk about your emotions in more detail.

- ∂ When you're experiencing strong emotions, decide what you want to do with them. Do you want to talk about them? Do you want to express them on your own through some creative means? Or do you prefer to do some physical exercise to vent them?

- ∂ At the end of your day, take some time to reflect on how you interacted with others. Were you more present in your thoughts, in your emotions or in your body? How do you know this?

- ∂ Keep a journal of some of your emotions and thoughts. In this way, you give them a tangible form and don't just think about them.

- ∂ Do some physical exercise or body-aware movement, like yoga, Tai Chi, Pilates or Qi Gong. You can also find some helpful exercises in chapter 02 (p. 14). These practices will help you be more in touch with your body.

- ∂ If you're usually sitting down at work, stand up and stretch multiple times a day so that you're not just present in your thinking but you also regularly activate your body.

- ∂ Practice meditation – it helps you step out of your thoughts and emotions and gain some perspective on yourself and life. Meditations that focus more on the body, such as the body scan in chapter 02 (p. 13), can be especially useful.

- ∂ When you feel caught up in your thoughts or emotions, practise intentional breathing exercises to be more present in your body. You can find such exercises in chapter 02 (p. 9).

The exercises that follow aim at helping you develop more awareness around your thinking and feeling dimensions and how these developed over time. They will also help you develop a more embodied way of striking a balance between both dimensions.

How it relates to your life

How does this text relate to your life?
Write down anything that comes to mind, heart or body.

Exercises

01. The thinker and feeler scale

ℽ   The scale below represents the spectrum between being a thinker (mainly engaged with your thoughts) and a feeler (mainly engaged with your emotions). Use a cross to mark where you believe you lie on the scale.

thinker   *feeler*

ℽ   Now, think of how you would prefer to be. Mark this on the scale below.

thinker   *feeler*

ℽ   Look at both scales and write down what you notice when you compare them. Is there such a big difference? How do you feel when you look at this comparison?

02. Who I am in different situations

♌ Think about the situations listed below. For each situation, ask yourself which aspect of yourself you tend to use most. Do you become more of a thinker and focus on your thoughts, a feeler and focus on your emotions or do you manage to strike a good balance between the two? Tick the appropriate box.

	Thinker	Balance	Feeler
Arguing with my partner			
Being in a physically unsafe situation			
Waiting before a job interview			
Losing someone important to me			
Going through a relationship breakup			
Receiving bad news			
Discussing a topic with a colleague			
Experiencing a financial setback			
Having a bad fight with a friend			
Receiving my exam results			
Arguing with my boss			

When you look at the above list, what do you observe about which situations engage more the thinking or the feeling part of yourself? Write down what this tells you about yourself. Can you think of other situations where you would act differently?

03. Tracking my thoughts and emotions

- During the following week, keep track of your emotions and thoughts.
- Use the table below to note down briefly what the situation was.
- Then, record what thoughts were going through your head.
- Finally, notice what emotions were present and rate the intensity of each emotion on a scale from 0 (none) to 10 (extremely intense).

Situation	My thoughts	My emotions and their intensity (0-10)
e.g. I forgot my keys at home.	*I'm so stupid!*	*Shame (3)* *Frustration (7)*

04. Framing my emotion

- The next time you notice you're strongly feeling an emotion, try being curious about it. Imagine what it might look like. Perhaps it looks like a person, an animal or something from fantasy. Perhaps it's just a shape, a colour or a mix of any of these.

- Use the space below to draw your emotion.

- Now, give a label to the emotion. You can use the lists in chapter 03 (p. 22) to help you.

ه You might want to repeat this with other emotions you experience. If so, grab some pieces of paper and repeat the exercise.

My Emotion: ___________________________

05. Feeling thoughts and emotions in my body

Notice a moment when you're primarily engaged with your thinking. Observe which parts of your body you can feel. Take note of whether it's a pleasant or an unpleasant sensation, or whether you experience numbness.

On the images below, use a green pen to shade the areas in your body where you notice a pleasant sensation. Use red to shade the areas where you notice an unpleasant sensation. Use blue to shade the areas that you feel are numb.

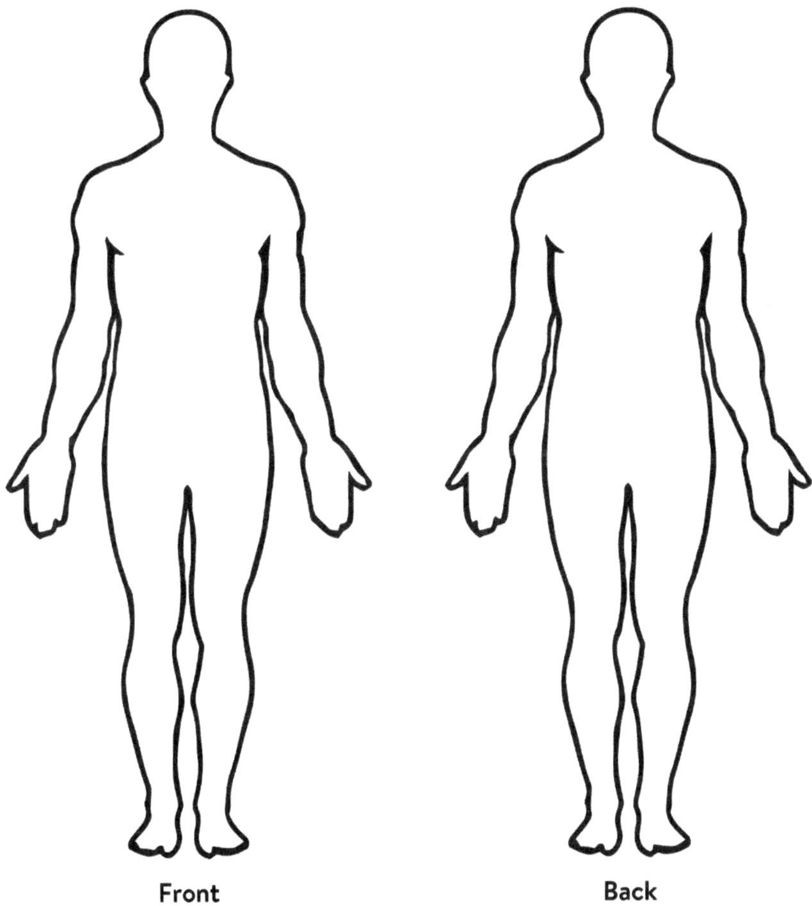

- Now, notice a moment when you're primarily engaged with your emotions. Notice which parts of your body you can feel. Take note of whether it's a pleasant or unpleasant sensation, or whether you experience any numbness.

- On the images below, use a green pen to shade the areas in your body where you notice a pleasant sensation. Use red to shade the areas where you notice an unpleasant sensation. Use blue to shade the areas that you feel are numb.

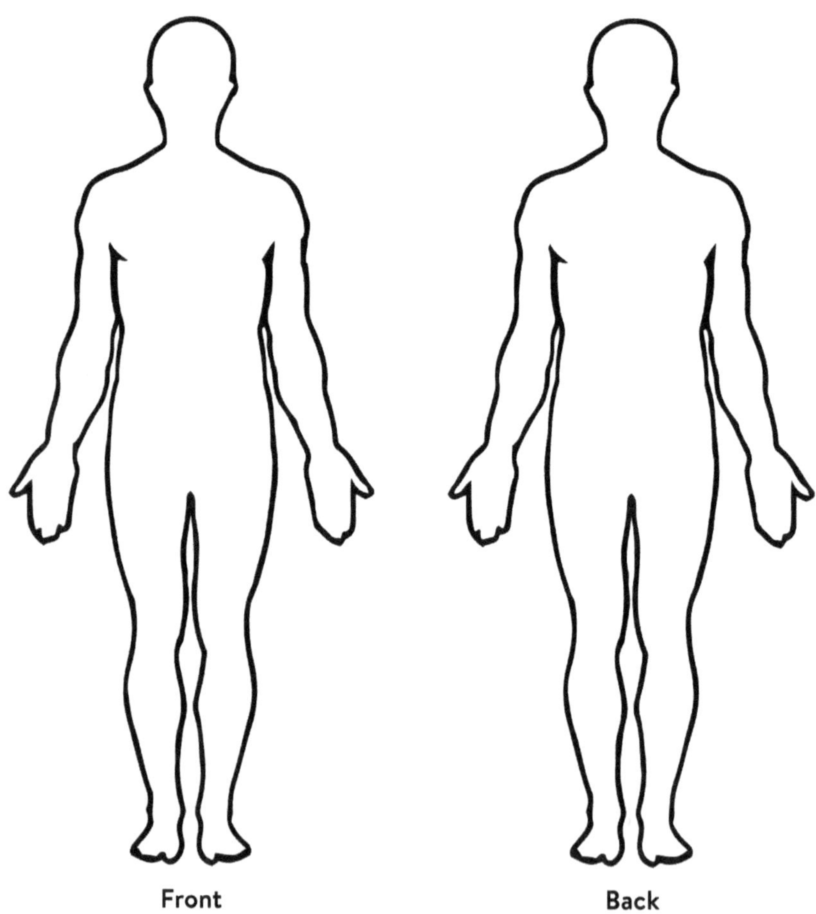

Front   **Back**

❧ Look at both drawings and take note of which parts of your body you're more connected with when you're engaged with your thoughts in contrast to when you're engaged with your emotions. Write down your observations.

06. My family's thinkers and feelers

∽   Think back to when you were a child and bring to mind your family
or other significant people who were around you. For each person,
use the scales below to mark how much of a thinker or a feeler they
were.

Person	Scale
	thinker ←————————————————→ feeler
	thinker ←————————————————→ feeler
	thinker ←————————————————→ feeler
	thinker ←————————————————→ feeler
	thinker ←————————————————→ feeler
	thinker ←————————————————→ feeler
	thinker ←————————————————→ feeler
	thinker ←————————————————→ feeler
	thinker ←————————————————→ feeler
	thinker ←————————————————→ feeler
	thinker ←————————————————→ feeler

- Look back at your own scale in exercise 01. Compare it with the scales you just marked for your family members. Who are you more similar to and different from? Does this tell you anything about how you became who you are?
- Write down what you've learnt from this exercise about how the members of your family impacted the way you now engage with your thoughts and emotions.

07. Emotional expression in my family

Take some time to recall how emotions were lived out in your family when you were young. Think about the following:

* Did people express their emotions?
* In what way?
* How was emotional expression viewed by different members of your family?

Write down your observations in the space below.

08. My opposite

- ❦ Imagine yourself as being the extreme opposite of who you are. If you mainly tend to focus on your thoughts, imagine yourself as an absolute feeler. And if you mainly engage with your emotions, imagine yourself as a total thinker.

- ❦ Imagine how you would speak, act and relate to others as that kind of person. Imagine how you would go about your work.

- ❦ Notice also what you like and dislike about being that kind of person and write it down in the table below.

What I like about my opposite	What I dislike about my opposite

- ❧ Now, choose one of the things that you like about your opposite. Think about how you can change something in the way you currently do things to develop this unexplored side of yourself.
- ❧ In the space below, write down what you want to change, how you plan on changing it and when you plan on taking action about it.

09. Changing my viewpoint

- If you notice that you're getting too emotional in a situation, leave the place where you are and go to a different location. The bathroom is often a very good option as it's a private place.

- Imagine that you're seeing the situation you were in from on top of a tall building.

- Notice how your emotion changes as you create distance between yourself and the situation.

- Write down what this exercise teaches you about how you can better deal with emotionally charged situations.

____

____

____

____

____

10. Breathing into the positive space

- Find a quiet place where you won't be disturbed.

- Mentally scan your body for any pleasant or calm sensation, small as it may be. Notice where it's located in your body.

- Focus on your breathing and imagine that your breath is reaching that pleasant place in your body.

- Every time you inhale, imagine that the pleasant sensation is expanding a bit.

- Repeat this for as long as you like. Maybe that pleasant sensation ends up extending to your entire body.

- Use this exercise to keep yourself in the present whenever you catch yourself being strongly caught up in your thoughts or emotions.

11. Checking in with my emotions

- For the coming week, set an alarm to ring every hour. Choose a gentle alarm sound, not one that startles you.

- Every time the alarm goes off, check what you're feeling. Use a word to label your emotion. You can use the list of emotions in chapter 03 (p. 22) to help you do this.

- Check what the intensity of the emotion is on a scale of 0 (none) to 10 (most intense).

- If the emotion is an unpleasant one, bring to mind someone who cares a lot for you and imagine what they would say to you in that particular moment. Note this down in the table below.

Emotion	Intensity (0-10)	What the caring person would say

Emotion	Intensity	What the person would say

 ✍ At the end of the week, look at your list of emotions. Write down your reflections about the different emotions you experienced. What are the statements that a loving person would tell you that you need to remember whenever you're struggling with your emotions?

12. **The passing clouds**

- Use this exercise when you're feeling overwhelmed by your thoughts or emotions.

- Sit or lie down comfortably and close your eyes. You can play some calming music in the background.

- Take a few deeper breaths and focus on how they reach deep inside your belly.

- Imagine that your thoughts or emotions are like clouds in the sky on a windy day. Observe how they come and go. Every time you get caught up in a feeling or thought, just notice it moving past you and fading away.

- Regularly check in with your breathing and notice any calmness or sense of being present that arises.
- Write down what you learnt from this exercise.

---

13. Shaking it off

- When you feel overwhelmed by your emotions or your thoughts, start jumping up and down and moving around chaotically.
- Put as much energy into this movement as possible. Imagine you're getting rid of the feeling of being overwhelmed by shaking it off.
- Keep on doing this until you feel physically exhausted.
- Now, sit or lie down comfortably and close your eyes.
- Check in with your breathing. It's probably quite heavy and rapid at this stage!

- Notice if there's any part of your body that feels more relaxed. Focus on it as your breathing calms down and notice how that sensation changes.
- Write down your observations about how movement helped you deal with feeling overwhelmed. How can you apply this exercise in your everyday life?

14. What the other is feeling

- Use this exercise when you're about to meet other people.
- During your interaction with them, make a conscious effort to think about what they're feeling. Come up with at least one emotion.
- Observe what made you think of that emotion. Was it anything about what the other person said, their tone of voice or their posture?

⁋ If it was difficult to come up with an emotion, try this exercise with someone you know well and check with them whether you guessed their emotion correctly.

⁋ In the space below, write down what you learnt about your awareness of other people's emotion and what helps you recognise it.

07

ON FEAR

An unexpected loud bang, being called to the head teacher's office after disrupting class, our partner threatening to break up with us, a snake winding itself towards us, our first performance on stage in front of an audience, a nurse with a syringe ready to prick our skin. There's a specific emotion that's triggered for many people in these situations: fear.

The aim of fear is to protect us from danger. It's a survival instinct deeply embedded in our brain that often bypasses our rational thinking. If we're in danger, we can't afford to waste time assessing what the danger actually is and coming up with a planned course of action. Instead, we need to act immediately.

Because the brain processes information about potential danger very rapidly, it often doesn't immediately distinguish between a real threat, like someone about to stab us, and an imagined threat, like the crawling sensation of a fly on our skin when we weren't expecting it. Our mind

Audio files for this chapter can be accessed at
thehorsesmouth.michaelconti.net/lbwy-ch07
or by scanning the adjacent QR code.

instantly reacts to what it perceives and activates the stress response. Our heart starts beating faster, our blood pressure increases, our breathing becomes more rapid, our chest feels tighter, our mouth dries up, our stomach feels upset and we start shaking.

Only after the stress response has been activated do we start rationally evaluating the situation and adjusting our reaction accordingly. At times, this makes us feel stupid as we realise that there wasn't anything to be afraid of in the first place. That light brushing sensation on our legs that made us jump up and scream was just a blade of grass, not the poisonous spider we thought it was! So, we end up letting go of our tension with a sigh or a laugh.

How fear develops

There are three ways in which fear develops in us.

The first is through instinct. This happens in situations where we immediately take action because our brain is physically wired to protect us from danger. An example of this is being startled by a loud bang.

The second is when we learn through our own experience what the things we need to be afraid of are. For example, we get bitten by a dog and we learn to be afraid of dogs, someone assaults us and we learn to fear that person.

The third is through other people teaching us what to fear. This is about how culture and society teach us whom and what to be afraid of. Some groups of people are judged as being dangerous regardless of reality. This, in turn, impacts how we feel about them. For example, some groups of migrants are seen as rapists, drug dealers or other kinds of criminals. Gay men are portrayed as bringing about the destruction of social order and as carriers of disease. And so we learn to be afraid of these groups of people.

Although we develop fear through our own experiences or what we're taught by others throughout our life, fear plays a particularly strong role when we're young. This is because, at that age, we're still learning about our environment. We're surrounded by a lot of things we know nothing about and we're still learning what is safe and what isn't. As time goes by, we learn to interpret our surroundings in a different way. We learn that darkness isn't, as such, something to be afraid of and that there aren't any ghosts or monsters lurking in the dark corner.

However, at times, some childhood fears can stick with us even when we grow older. These fears that we experienced when we were younger end up embedding themselves deeply inside our mind. This can be because of something terrible that actually happened to us, like being bullied by another group of children. Or it can be that, as kids, we interpreted something as being a dangerous thing and this interpretation stuck with us right through to adulthood. For example, if when we were young we were told that spiders are poisonous, our minds might have interpreted that in a generalised way and concluded that "A spider will try to bite me and it will kill me!" As a result, we get stuck with that interpretation even though we're now adults!

When fear becomes excessive

There are, however, times when some of us experience excessive fear of an object or event, or we experience a lot of anxiety around it. At times, we can acknowledge that our reaction is disproportionate and irrational. And yet, we cannot stop ourselves from being caught up in the overwhelming fear that takes over and paralyses us. We rush out of the room if we see a small spider, we're unable to stand on a chair out of fear of falling or we cannot tolerate being inside a lift. These fears of objects or situations have become a *phobia*.

Phobias often develop in childhood or teenage years. One way in which we develop a phobia is when we witness that fear at home, like if we have a parent who has a phobia of flying or of being in a constricted space.

But phobias can also develop as a result of our direct experience of something negative. In this case, we can develop a phobia that's directly related to the event. For example, if we were attacked by a cat, we might develop a phobia of cats later on in life.

Our mind can also connect the negative event with something else that was present at that moment but wasn't directly related to the event. For example, if we were assaulted by a gang in the street, we might develop a fear of public spaces.

Another thing that can happen is that, when we experience a negative event, we feel helpless in front of that fear and so it ends up being displaced onto something completely unrelated. For example, being a victim of sexual abuse can often be accompanied by the experience of fear. However, given that we have no control over that abuse taking place, we can end up feeling a strong sense of helplessness. Our mind wishes that we could avoid what's making us afraid. However, it also knows that we can't avoid it. These conflicting thoughts put us in a very uncomfortable psychological situation. As a result, we might displace that fear onto something else that we can have tangible control over and so develop an 'unrelated' phobia, such as a fear of snakes, vomiting or water. Because of this displacement, our mind plays a trick on itself. Trying to control the phobia gives us a sense of being in control. This feeling is then displaced onto other areas of life, including what's actually making us afraid in the first place. It gives us the illusion that we can, in some way, be in control of the abuse that we're experiencing.

Being fearless

Given that fear tries to protect us from danger and vulnerability, it often activates the stress response and so, at times, it can be a very disabling emotion. However, some of us react to fear-generating situations in the opposite way – we act as if we're fearless. The reality is that no one is actually fearless unless they have a neurological problem, as fear is essential for ensuring survival. The only thing that we can do is to suppress fear. But, in doing so, we risk losing touch with our body and with our in-built mechanism that protects us from danger.

So, why do some of us still try to suppress fear? By acting as if we have no fear, we try to overcome the helplessness that accompanies feeling afraid. This helplessness can be even more terrifying for us than the real danger we're encountering. It's a helplessness that might have resulted from trauma or from a negative self-image. Whenever it's activated, we end up trying to overcompensate for it. We play the role of the invincible person, the tough one, the person who can take on anything. But, ultimately, what we're actually doing is trying to shelter our vulnerability from others and from ourselves.

The positive side of fear

Both being fearful and acting as if we have no fear are two extreme ways of dealing with fear. By getting to know and respecting our fear, we can be better informed about what we need to do in a specific situation. Fear helps us focus and be more aware of what's happening in our environment. It helps us plan for negative eventualities. What we need to learn is how to be less afraid and take more reasonable control of our lives instead of letting fear decide for us.

How to learn to fear less

The following are some suggestions to help you live out a more balanced approach in relation to your fear.

- Take some time to understand your fear. What triggers it? How does your body react when you're feeling afraid and what thoughts come to mind? What are you afraid might happen? What soothes you when you're afraid?

- When you feel afraid, instead of just saying that you feel afraid, name what it is that you're feeling afraid of. Say to yourself: "I'm afraid of [what you're afraid of] ." or "I'm afraid that … [what you're afraid could happen] ."

- Try gaining some perspective on your fear. Is it really as bad as you fear? What could be a more realistic way of viewing things?

- Visualise being successful in something you're afraid of doing. Mentally rehearse this image. This provides your mind with another scenario of how things can be rather than have your imagination dictated to by fear.

- Imagine you are your best friend or an encouraging parent. What would you tell yourself if you saw yourself feeling afraid? Say this aloud to yourself.

- Use humour. A good laugh releases tension and diminishes the effect of the stress response.

- Find ways to ground yourself in the present. Use breathing exercises, focus on relaxing your body or practise mindfulness. You can find some of these exercises in chapter 02.

❧   When feeling afraid, act in the opposite way to how your fear pushes you to behave. Immerse yourself in what terrifies you or gradually expose yourself to it – but get there. You might want to sit with your fear for 2-3 minutes at a time, take a break and then go back to it.

❧   Be proud of yourself when you overcome fear and ensure that you give yourself some form of reward.

❧   Grow in other areas of life so you can meet new challenges. This will help you feel more empowered in general.

❧   If there are phobias that are affecting your life, speak to a professional who can provide additional help to manage them.

The exercises that follow aim at helping you develop more awareness of your fear, further understand where it comes from and explore how you might manage your fear in a better way.

How it relates to your life

How does this text relate to your life?
Write down anything that comes to mind, heart or body.

Exercises

01. My greatest fears

- In the table below, make a list of your fears, big or small.
- In the second column, rate these fears from 1 (lowest level of fear) to 10 (highest level of fear).

List of fears	Rating (1-10)

02. Drawing my fear

- Imagine your fear as an entity external to you. It could be a person, animal, object or shape. It could be real or imaginary.

- Make a drawing of it in the space below.

My Fear

- Look at your drawing. What does it tell you about your fear? Does it show you anything about how you relate to it?
- Write down what you learnt about your fear.

03. My fears when I was younger

- Bring to mind when you were still a child or a teenager.
- Think about the following questions:
  - What were you scared of back then?
  - What has happened to those fears?
  - Are they still around?
  - Have they transformed into something else?
- Write down these memories and your observations of how things have changed for you in relation to fear.

04. How others handled fear

- Bring to mind your childhood home and the people who were present: parents, siblings or other adults.
- Think about how they handled fear:
  - Were they more of the fearful or the fearless kind of person?
  - What were they afraid of?
  - What did you learn from them about how to deal with fearful situations?
- Note down your reflections about what you witnessed around you and how this influenced your relationship with fear.

05. The most daring thing I did

- Think of the most daring thing that you've ever done.

- Close your eyes and replay it in your mind.

- Pay attention to any emotions that arise for you. Notice if any physical sensations come up as well.

- Think about your reaction to this most daring thing you ever did. What does your reaction tell you about how you handle fear today? Have you become more or less afraid since then?

- Write down what you've learnt about the way you react to situations that bring up fear and any changes you've noticed in this regard throughout your life.

06. My body and fear

- Look at the list in exercise 01. Choose one of the fears that you scored at 7 or above.

- Find a comfortable position, preferably sitting or lying down.

- Now, close your eyes and imagine being in that situation. Play it out in your mind.

- Notice what's happening in your body. Where can you feel the fear in your body? Are you holding any tension physically?

- Now, check with yourself whether you wish to adopt a different posture as a result of getting in touch with your fear. Go ahead and shift your posture.

- Again, notice where you feel the fear in your body. This time, amplify the posture you adopted. For example, if you first felt like crouching, this time curl up in a ball until you cannot make yourself any smaller. Or, if you first felt like turning your face away, now turn away your whole torso or body.

- Stay for a while in this final posture, taking note of your emotions and any physical sensations that arise.

- After some time, start doing the opposite movement by opening up that part of your body that turned away from fear. For example, if you were curled up, open up your arms and back. Or if you had turned away, turn back to 'confront' your fear face-to-face with your hands on your hips.

- Stay in this new posture for a while. Notice how it feels different to be facing your fear in this way.

- Write down what you learnt about the relationship between fear and your body. How does fear affect it? And how does the feeling of fear change when you use your body in a different way?

07. "I'm not afraid!"

- ✍ Bring to mind something or someone that makes you feel afraid. Imagine it/them in front of you. If it's an event, imagine it happening while you're watching it.

- ✍ Notice your posture and any feeling of tension that might arise.

- ✍ Now, adopt one of the power poses shown below. Take some deep breaths and observe what it feels like to assume that pose.

- While staying in the power pose, keep in mind the thing you're afraid of and address it while saying aloud: "I'm not afraid!"

- Repeat the previous step and increase the volume of your voice until you feel that you're making use of all the power you have.

- ❧ Relax from your power pose and imagine the person, object or situation again. Do you notice any difference in how you're now feeling in relation to them?
- ❧ Note down your reflections about how you can use your body posture to better confront your fears.

08. Connecting to my anger

- Start this exercise by standing in front of a mattress or some cushions.

- Picture one of your fears, preferably one that really bothers you and you want to get rid of.

- Think about how that fear is adversely impacting and limiting your life and how it's generating negativity in you.

- With every inhale, allow yourself to connect to a feeling of anger towards that fear because of how it's affecting you. Clench your fists and tense your hands and forearms for a few minutes as you try to connect to that anger.

- Imagine that your mattress or bunch of cushions represents that fear.

- Using your forearms rather than your hands (to avoid injury), unleash your anger towards the fear by hitting out at the mattress or cushions as hard as you can. While doing so, allow yourself to exhale loudly or to shout out your anger towards your fear.

- The next time you feel fear, connect to your anger. Does it shift anything in your determination to overcome it and to take action?

- Write down your observations and reflections from this exercise.

09. My less-afraid self

- Find a comfortable posture, preferably sitting down.

- Explore how your body feels when you use a soothing caress. Maybe you can gently stroke your face, palms, chest or thighs. Check which movement feels most comforting.

- Close your eyes and imagine that in front of you stands a version of yourself that's much less afraid than you usually are. Imagine what that version of yourself looks like, how it stands and speaks.

- If that version of yourself could talk to you about your fears in order to reassure you, encourage you or soothe you, what would it say? Imagine it speaking to you while you perform the soothing gesture you were using before. Hear it tell you "It's OK! It's OK to be afraid. But you're also strong and don't need to fear so much. I'm here for you, with you, supporting you."

- In the space below, note down anything significant that came up for you during this exercise. Think of how you can use this inner voice or the soothing gesture to deal with moments when you feel afraid.

10. A letter to my fearful part

∽   Write a letter to that part of yourself that often feels afraid. Use the space below to write it or grab another sheet of paper so you can have a physical copy of it rather than a digital one.

∽   While writing your letter, can you be gentle towards that part of yourself? What can you say to it in a kind and reassuring manner? Aim at showing a lot of understanding and encouragement.

11. Protecting the fearful part

- Go back to exercise 02, where you drew your fear.

- Imagine something that you could add to the drawing so as to protect that fearful part of yourself and add this to your drawing.

- Look at your drawing with the changes you just made to it. How does it feel to see your fearful part protected?

- Note down any reflections that come up for you from this exercise.

12. Breaking it down

- Look at your list of fears in exercise 01.

- Choose the one with the lowest score.

- Think of how you can gradually approach that fear by breaking it down into tiny, doable tasks. For example, if you're afraid of going on a rollercoaster, you might think of the following steps:

1. Picture yourself looking up at a rollercoaster while it's standing still.
2. Picture yourself looking up at the rollercoaster while it's moving.
3. Picture yourself looking up at the rollercoaster while you're in the queue waiting to ride it.
4. Picture yourself sitting on the rollercoaster before it starts moving.
5. Picture yourself on the rollercoaster while it's moving.
6. Go to an actual funfair and stand next to the rollercoaster you find the easiest.
7. While standing next to the rollercoaster, picture yourself on it while it's standing still and then when it's moving.
8. Go to stand next to a rollercoaster you find more difficult.
9. Picture yourself on this rollercoaster when it's standing still and then when it's moving.
10. Stand in the queue for the rollercoaster you find the easiest and, when it's your turn to board it, leave the queue.
11. Stand in the queue and, this time, board it.
12. Try a rollercoaster you find more difficult.

❧ In the space below, write down the fear you want to tackle and brainstorm the small tasks you need to take to overcome it. Arrange them in sequence from the easiest to the hardest.

---

13. Taking action

- ✑ Look at the first task on your list in exercise 12. Use the table below to make a plan of when and where you're going to take action in order to overcome your fear.

- ✑ Before you engage with the task, rate your fear on a scale of 0 (none) to 10 (maximum).

- ✑ Engage in the task. Afterwards, recall what your fear was during the task and rate this on a scale of 0 to 10.

- ✑ Focus on how afraid you're feeling now, after you've engaged with the task. Again, rate your fear from 0 to 10. Do you notice any change in your levels of fear?

- ✑ Decide on whether you want to repeat the same task to lower your fear score or whether you want to engage in a task that's a bit more difficult. Be gentle with yourself. Don't overdo it as this would re-trigger your fear! But be firm as well and don't let your fear dictate everything!

ℝ Feel free to stop at any of the steps you've planned – only you know when you've reached your limit for the day. You can always continue another time. After you stop, make sure that you reward yourself with something you enjoy. You deserve it!

When and where	Task	Fear score before (0-10)	Fear score during (0-10)	Fear score after (0-10)

When & where	Task	Score before	Score during	Score after

- ✍ Reflect on how your fear changed in relation to each task you set for yourself. What does this teach you about handling your fears?
- ✍ Write down your reflections below.

08

ON BEING ANGRY

What does the word 'anger' evoke in you? What immediate thoughts and feelings come to mind? Is anger very much present in your life or is it something you avoid? Do you come from a culture where it's acceptable to express your anger or is such emotional expression disapproved of? How does this affect you?

Anger is about feeling antagonism towards someone or something. It's not the same as aggression. Aggression is an action. It's something we have control over. In contrast, anger is an emotion and as an emotion we have no control over whether we feel it or not. The function of anger is to protect us against being hurt. When we feel threatened or powerless or when we feel that we run the risk of being so, we get angry. When we feel angry, our fight mode is activated so we defend ourselves and fight back against what we feel is threatening us. This threat could be a physical one, like when someone bumps into us or intentionally hits us.

Audio files for this chapter can be accessed at **thehorsesmouth.michaelconti.net/lbwy-ch08** *or by scanning the adjacent QR code.*

But it can also be emotional or psychological, such as when we're deceived, disrespected, invalidated, treated unfairly, ignored or when things don't go according to plan. Hence, anger is quite a complex emotion and its intensity can vary a lot, leading us to experience anything from mild displeasure to extreme rage.

What anger consists of

Anger is an emotional reaction made up of three components.

The trigger

The trigger is the threat that we perceive, something that 'pushes our button'. It's usually what we deem to be the cause of our anger, like when someone tramples on our foot.

Our emotional or physical state

This refers to what we're feeling and physically sensing when the trigger happens. If we're feeling relaxed and someone accidentally tramples on our foot, we probably won't take any particular notice of it even though we might not like it. However, if we're feeling very tired or anxious, or we're already angry because of something else, having our foot trampled on can easily send us flying into a burst of rage.

Our interpretation

Our mind is constantly interpreting and judging situations. If it considers a situation to be blameworthy and punishable, it will react with anger. If we assume there was an intention – usually a negative one – behind the threatening action and if we see ourselves as the intended target, then that action is bound to trigger even more anger. Using the previous example, if someone tramples on our foot and we think that they did this on purpose, we will feel directly attacked and we will react very angrily towards them. If, on the other hand, we assume that it was a mistake, it's more likely that we end up dismissing it and continuing with whatever we were doing.

We tend to experience anger as a very uncomfortable emotion. This is because our threat response gets activated. Adrenaline is released into our blood bringing about numerous changes in our body. For example, our muscles will tense more, our heart will beat faster and our blood pressure will increase. These changes feel physically uncomfortable. They make us feel like we're losing control and this makes us fear what might happen next.

What influences how we experience anger?

One thing that influences how we experience anger is current situations in our life. If our job is generating anger and that anger builds up inside us, it can easily be displaced onto other areas of our life, such as our relationships. We might end up getting angry over trivial things at home. But what's actually happening is that our accumulated stress from work is being released at home. Anger can also be triggered by situations of loss, like when we're mourning someone's death or when we go through a relationship breakup.

Past experiences also influence how we experience anger. If we've been subject to abuse, trauma, bullying or similar situations, we probably have a lot of anger built up inside us. Similarly to what was mentioned above, the negative emotional charge that has been stored inside us is discharged when it's triggered by things that are happening today. This can result in the release of a disproportionate amount of anger.

A final thing that strongly influences how we experience anger today is our childhood and upbringing. We might have been brought up in environments where anger was acted out aggressively. We learnt that any form of expression of anger is normal and acceptable. As a result, we have no real understanding of anger and we simply switch from what triggers our emotion to aggressive behaviour. On the other hand, we might have been brought up in an environment where we weren't allowed to express our disapproval. Caregivers might have punished us for expressing our anger or our cultural and religious beliefs viewed the expression of anger in a negative light. This might have made us feel guilty about feeling angry and so we learnt to suppress our anger. For some of us, anger might have meant being a target of, or witness to, harm and destruction. For example, it might have been commonplace for one of our caregivers to fly into a rage and start screaming at us or become aggressive towards their partner. In such cases, we learn that anger is a dangerous emotion as it only results in people getting hurt. We learn that it's an emotion we need to avoid at all costs.

What happens when we suppress our anger?

The problem with suppressing anger is that it doesn't actually go away. Instead, it builds up inside us but outside of our awareness. One of the consequences of this is that the anger gets directed at ourselves. We develop a very critical self, we engage in self-harming behaviours or we shut ourselves off from the world. The emotional charge of the anger we suppress often gets locked into our body. We start experiencing medically unexplainable shoulder tensions, back pain, headaches and high blood pressure. We might even end up suffering from chronic physical conditions.

Another consequence of suppressing anger is that we turn down the intensity of all our emotions. This is a case of 'better safe than sorry', where we shut down or diminish the intensity of all our emotions to ensure that anger doesn't come to the surface. It's like flooding a room with water to prevent it from catching fire. There will definitely not be any fire, but the room will also be very wet and cold! In such situations, we end up feeling depressed, a sign that all our emotions are being inhibited.

Yet another consequence of suppressing anger is that we experience moments when we unexpectedly feel overwhelmed with anger. We experience this like a huge surge of negative energy that takes us by surprise as it rushes through us. We erupt like a volcano. When this happens, it's next to impossible to notice the gradual changes that signal to us that we're getting angry. Instead, we experience a change from zero to a hundred. From being in a relatively calm state, we suddenly fly into a rage. The change can be so strong that we might be unable to remember what actually happened when we 'saw red'.

Anger as a substitute emotion

Until now we've spoken about anger as an emotional reaction to threat. However, anger can also act as a substitute emotion. Pain, fear and vulnerability make us experience a deep sense of powerlessness. This evokes the freeze response where our psychological defences collapse in front of threat. However, should anger step in, it activates the fight response and we feel a sense of empowerment. In this way, anger becomes a distraction from the emotions of pain, fear and vulnerability that we're experiencing and can lead us to hold onto a sense of righteousness and superiority. Although this reaction can be useful, at times, it can still lead to the suppression of other emotions.

Can anger be a good thing?

Anger *is* a strong and intense emotion. Like fire, unless handled well, it *can* be very destructive. However, the destruction doesn't lie in the feeling of anger itself but in how we express it. If handled well, anger can actually be hugely beneficial. It protects us from being taken advantage of, it helps us feel empowered, it motivates us to establish safety for ourselves and for others we care about. After all, it's anger that makes it possible to stand up against bullies, to fight for the rights of those we love and to struggle against injustice. The challenge consists in finding the right balance between connecting to the anger and expressing it in a forceful, but non-destructive, way.

How to prevent anger from blowing up

There are three main ways we can help ourselves manage anger so that it doesn't result in destructive outbursts. Soothing techniques aim at calming down the anger by helping us enter into a state of relaxation. Venting techniques help to let out the anger and so reduce the internal emotional pressure. Expressive techniques allow anger to be channelled and expressed more constructively. The following are some examples of these techniques. In the case of both the venting and expressive techniques, it's important to have time to relax afterwards or to use one of the soothing techniques. Otherwise, there's a risk of just amplifying the feeling of anger.

Soothing techniques

- When you feel anger building up, stretch your body, pull your shoulders back and do some neck rolls. This helps relax your tense muscles and encourages your emotions to calm down.
- Use relaxation techniques, such as breathing exercises, meditation or yoga. You can find examples of these in chapter 02.
- Use humour to tone down the anger or find something that makes you laugh. Laughter can often be the best medicine!
- Listen to relaxing music that takes your focus away from the anger.

Venting techniques

- Do some intense physical exercise. This can be a good way of burning off the extra energy that builds up as a result of anger.
- Listen to music with heavy beats and dance to it. Let your anger turn into physical movement and shake it off.
- Write down your angry feelings in a journal. This helps give a tangible form to your feelings and provides an opportunity to express them freely and safely.

Expressive techniques

- Take some time to think before you speak. Anger can lead you to be impulsive and you can't take back what you say. So, pause before saying something and check if you might end up regretting what you're about to say.
- Focus your energies on coming up with a solution to the problem. Here you can constructively use your anger rather than feeling defeated and getting stuck.
- Improve your communication skills. Listen more attentively to others as that will help you understand them better and stop you from misinterpreting their actions. Learn to voice your anger in a firm, but non-aggressive, way to avoid it from building up.

The exercises that follow help increase your ability to get more in touch with your anger and understand it. They will also help you find ways of working through your anger without it becoming destructive.

How it relates to your life

How does this text relate to your life?
Write down anything that comes to mind, heart or body.

Exercises

01. The signs of anger

- Notice a moment when you're feeling angry.
- Use the list below to check whether you notice any of the physical, emotional or behavioural signs indicated.

Physical

- Increased heart rate
- Clenched jaws or teeth-grinding
- Tightness in chest or belly
- Tension in shoulders, neck or back
- Clenched hands
- Other muscular tension
- Frowning
- Stomach-churning
- Shaking or trembling
- Weakness in the legs
- Feeling faint
- Feeling hot
- Sweating

Emotional

- Anxious or nervous
- Easily irritated
- Guilty
- Sad or depressed
- Resentful
- Humiliated
- Wanting to strike out physically or verbally

Behavioural

- Pacing up and down
- Being sarcastic
- Shouting, yelling, screaming or crying
- Losing your sense of humour
- Acting in an abusive manner
- Craving substances such as alcohol, tobacco or drugs

ৼ Write down what you learnt from this exercise about how anger tends to manifest itself in you.

---

02. My angry thoughts

ৼ The next time you feel angry, take note of what you start thinking right after you experience the anger. Do you start blaming someone? Do you take that action personally? What story do you make up in your mind about why that person did what they did?

ৼ Also take note of what happens to your anger while you're having these thoughts. Does it decrease, stay as it is or get more intense?

ৼ Write down your reflections about how your thoughts and feelings of anger affect each other.

03. Monitoring my anger

- Over the coming week or two, notice when you feel angry. For each situation, try answering the following questions:
  - What was the situation that triggered the anger and who was involved?
  - How were you feeling just before you got angry (e.g. tired, irritable, anxious)?
  - What were you thinking while you were feeling angry?
  - If you expressed your anger, how did you do it?
  - If you did not express your anger but, instead, kept it inside you, what did you notice about your behaviour or physical sensations?
  - What was the outcome of feeling angry?
- Use the table below to keep track of each situation.

The situation and my initial feelings & sensations	My thoughts while feeling angry	My behaviour while feeling angry	My physical sensations while feeling angry	Outcome of feeling angry

<table>
<tr><td></td><td></td><td></td><td></td><td></td></tr>
<tr><td></td><td></td><td></td><td></td><td></td></tr>
<tr><td></td><td></td><td></td><td></td><td></td></tr>
</table>

∽ Look back at the table you completed. What have you learnt about yourself from this exercise?

04. Creating an anger scale

∾ The following are some words used to describe different intensities of anger. Use the scale below to write down these words according to the intensity of anger that they represent for you. Start on the left side with those words that signify the lowest intensity of anger and finish on the right side with those that signify the highest intensity of anger. If you feel that some words are of the same intensity, write them next to each other.

∾ When you feel angry, use these words to better express your level of anger.

← ·· →

lowest intensity of anger   *highest intensity of anger*

Words that express different levels of anger

∾ Angry	∾ Furious
∾ Annoyed	∾ Hostile
∾ Bitter	∾ Impatient
∾ Cross	∾ Infuriated
∾ Displeased	∾ Irritated
∾ Enraged	∾ Outraged
∾ Exasperated	∾ Resentful
∾ Frustrated	∾ Wound up

05. Clenching and releasing

- Start clenching your hands and tensing your forearm muscles.

- Notice how your sensation changes as you build up the tension. Take note of any emotions you start feeling.

- Expand the tension to your upper arms and shoulders. Contract the muscles in your face and make an angry facial expression.

- Keep all these muscles tense for about 5 to 10 minutes.

- Notice where in your body you primarily experience a build-up of energy.

- Observe what the emotions you're feeling are or any thoughts that cross your mind.

- Check what has happened to your breathing. How often and how deeply are you breathing now?

- Now, relax all your muscles. Open your face wide and release your hands and arms. Take some slow, deep breaths.

- What do you notice about that build-up of energy now? And what do you notice about your emotions?

- Write down your reflections about what happens to you when there's a build-up of tension and what happens when you release that tension. Focus on your breathing, your emotions, your thoughts and any sensations in your body.

06. Creatively expressing anger

⤳ Give your anger a tangible form by drawing it in the space below. If you prefer, use other creative ways of expressing it – create some music or give shape to a lump of clay!

My Anger

- When you look at, or listen to, your expression of anger, what feelings come up in relation to it? What would you like to do with your expressed anger?
- Write about the experience of giving your anger a tangible form.

07. How anger was handled in my past

- Take some time to think about the following questions:
    - How was anger perceived and handled in your family and at school?
    - What about your community or society?
    - What about your groups of friends?
    - How were you taught about whether it's OK, or not, to feel and express anger? In what way were you taught this?

Write down your reflections on how you learnt about experiencing and expressing anger.

Write down your reflections on how you learnt about experiencing and expressing anger.

08. When I got angry

- ✍ Use the table below to make a list of the events in your life that you feel angry about.

- ✍ Find a place where you won't be disturbed. Go through each item on your list and picture it in your head.

- ✍ Notice any thoughts and emotions that come up. Do you sense any change in your body while you're thinking about them?

- ✍ Use the table below to note down what you felt or thought about each of these events in your life.

Event	Feelings, thoughts and sensations

09. "I should not feel ashamed or guilty!"

√ Did you ever feel ashamed of, or guilty about, feeling angry? If so, imagine that the shame or guilt could speak. What would it be saying to you? Write this down in the space below.

____

____

____

____

____

____

____

____

____

____

____

____

____

____

____

√ Now, stand in front of a mirror. Read what you've just written down. Then say aloud to yourself: "I shouldn't feel guilty or ashamed about feeling angry. Anger is a completely normal emotion!"

√ What does it feel like to say this aloud? Did you manage to maintain eye contact with your reflection or did you avoid it?

- ⋘ Try repeating this a few times, each time increasing the energy and power of what you're saying by increasing the strength and volume of your voice and by looking at yourself in the eye.
- ⋘ Write down your reflections about any changes you noticed in yourself after this exercise and any difficulties you encountered.

10. How I channel my anger

- If you feel that you rarely get angry, can you think of other ways in which you might be channelling your anger or what you might be doing to shut it down? Maybe you experience violent fantasies or you become passive aggressive with others. Maybe you withdraw when you're around other people or you channel your anger into sex. Maybe you drown it in alcohol or in drugs, or maybe you have other ways of doing it.

- Write down your observations about how you channel your anger.

11. Sitting in front of my anger

- Find a space where you won't be disturbed and place two chairs in front of each other.

- Sit on one of them and imagine that your anger is sitting in the chair opposite you. Imagine what it looks like and how it's sitting in relation to you.

- How do you physically feel and what emotions come up when you look at your anger?

- Check with yourself if you want to readjust your chair or your posture in relation to it.

- Allow yourself 5 to 10 minutes to say anything you want to your anger. Maybe you're more understanding towards it, or you're angry at it or ashamed of it. Just allow yourself to speak freely without censoring yourself.

- When you're done, take a couple of minutes to note how you feel now that you've expressed yourself to your anger.

- Now, get up from your chair and go and sit in the opposite one. Imagine that you've left yourself behind and that you've now become solely your feeling of anger. Bring to mind what you've just said to your anger. While being your own anger, how do you feel hearing this being said to you? What does it make you want to do or say?

- Take a few minutes to speak back to yourself, only talking as if you are your anger.

- When you're done, pause and take a few moments to notice what it feels like to have expressed yourself as your own anger.

- Now, go and sit again in the first chair you were sitting in. Close your eyes for a moment and feel the chair underneath you and your feet flat on the ground. You're now yourself again with your anger still sitting in front of you.

- Recall what your angry self said to you. How do you feel about it? What physical sensations come up when you replay it in your head? Check whether you want to now shift your posture or the position of your chair in relation to the other chair where anger is sitting.

- Speak back to your angry self for the last time.

- Finally, close your eyes and imagine your anger getting up from the other chair and leaving the room you're in. Take a few deep breaths and notice how it feels to be yourself again, alone in the room.

- Write down your reflections about this exercise. What did you learn about your anger and your relationship with it? Did anything shift in the way you usually perceive, or relate to, it?

12. Free to be angry

- ✍ Find a space where you're undisturbed. Preferably do this exercise while standing up.

- ✍ Recall a situation that makes you feel angry.

- ✍ Picture yourself unleashing your anger. What would you do if you had the freedom to do anything you felt like doing? Let your imagination run wild for a while. Try not to block yourself – thinking about it doesn't mean that you'll end up doing it!

- ✍ Take a couple of deep breaths and start moving your body as if its movement is being directed by your anger. You might flail your arms, jump up and down, make chopping gestures or try to push the air in front of you away from you. Allow the movement to build up and intensify over time. Allow that movement to continue until you feel that you've vented all the energy that was inside you.

- Now, bring your movement to a standstill and take a few slower, deeper breaths.

- Recall the initial situation again. If you still feel anger coming up, repeat the steps above.

- When you're done, focus on your feet pushing into the ground. Feel all of your weight pushing down into your legs, into your feet and into the ground. Feel the support of the ground as it pushes back your feet. Take a few deep breaths, imaging the air reaching all the way down to your feet.

- Finally, let your body loosen up a bit. Gently sway from side to side and back to front, allowing yourself to come to the centre again and connect to the present moment.

- Write down what you learnt from this exercise about how easily you allow yourself to express anger. Did you allow it to become physical? What did it feel like? Was it helpful? If you didn't allow it to become physical, what stopped you?

13. Chaotic dancing

- Find a piece of music that sounds angry or chaotic.

- Play the music, setting the volume as loud as possible in the place you're in.

- Allow yourself to move or dance in the most chaotic way possible. You can also yell out any utterances or words that express the energy inside you. Avoid censoring yourself.

- Take note of how you felt after the music ended. How can this exercise help you release your anger?

14. Hitting the air

- The next time you feel angry, find a place where you're alone.

- Imagine that what is angering you is right in front of you.

- Form your hands into fists and start punching the air in front of you or hold your forearms and hands in a straight line and do martial art-like gestures by slashing the air in front of you. Imagine that you're attacking what's making you angry.

- If possible, do this while breathing out very loudly and making a sound. You could shout out "Aaah!" very quickly with every arm movement you make. Feel that sound coming out from your abdomen!

- When you feel that the energy has subsided, hold yourself still either sitting or standing. Remember that anger is a normal reaction but that now you have the choice as to how to behave towards other people and yourself.

- Take a few longer and slower breaths until you feel calmer.
- Write down your reflections about this exercise, any obstacles you encountered while doing it and how it can be of use in your life.

15. Shaking it off

- When you feel angry, find a place where you're undisturbed.

- Stand up straight with your feet hip-width apart.

- Start bending and straightening your legs from the knee and ankle as if the ground beneath you is starting to slowly vibrate up and down. For now, just allow your legs to shake.

- Slowly allow that shaking to include your hips as well, then let it move up to your torso, your arms and hands, your neck and your head.

- Let the vibrations increase in speed and strength while ensuring that you don't strain your neck in the process. Imagine that these waves of energy going through your body are your anger that's being shaken off. Allow yourself to really shake and vibrate!

- Finally, let the vibrations subside and bring yourself to a still, upright position. Notice the calmness or sense of release that you're feeling. Notice your feet firmly planted on the ground as you bring yourself back to the present moment.

- Write about what you experienced during this exercise and how it can help you deal with anger.

16. Planning calmer moments

    If you tend to be very explosive with your anger, try to identify which people or areas in your life help you feel calmer or more relaxed. List these down in the space below.

∽ Make it a point to engage with at least one of them each day throughout this coming week. Every time you do this, check how you feel afterwards and note this down below.

Day	What I did	How I felt afterwards

09

ON SHAME AND GUILT

Shame and guilt are two burdens that most of us start carrying very early on in life and continue doing so throughout most of our lifetime. They can prevent us from living a happier and more fulfilled life. Guilt is predominantly a feeling that we did something wrong. We feel guilty having offended someone or having stolen or damaged something. Shame is more to do with who we are and how we judge ourselves. It's seeing ourselves as fundamentally flawed and unworthy.

Guilt

Guilt is about feeling emotionally uncomfortable regarding having done something wrong. There's a positive side to guilt because it can stop us from doing things that harm others. In this way, it makes it possible to respect each other and to live together in a society. If I damage someone

Audio files for this chapter can be accessed at
thehorsesmouth.michaelconti.net/lbwy-ch09
or by scanning the adjacent QR code.

else's car while driving, this will negatively affect how they feel and it will cost them money to repair it. Such an event can lead me to feel that I did something wrong and so I feel guilty. This might push me to contact the car owner, make my apologies and make amends. There are other situations where one cannot make up for the damage inflicted or the hurt that was caused, such as when someone is betrayed. However, owning up to one's mistakes and asking for forgiveness can allow for healing to take place for everyone involved.

Despite this, guilt can also have an unhelpful side to it. At times, we can feel psychologically uncomfortable because we believe we did something wrong according to unrealistically high standards we impose upon ourselves. Examples of these include forgetting to put out the trash when it was our turn to do so or arriving a few minutes late for an appointment with a friend. In such cases, the guilt that we feel can be disproportionate to what happened. Everybody forgets to take out the trash at times and arriving late can happen to anyone. In these situations, guilt does not help us change our behaviour. It only serves for us to punish ourselves.

Guilt can also be unhelpful when we've done something wrong but we continue holding onto the sense of guilt long past the moment when we asked for forgiveness. For example, we might have said something hurtful to our partner in a moment when we were feeling angry. It was hurtful and out of place and we genuinely asked for forgiveness. But we cannot undo the past. So, if we continue feeling guilty for a long time after that, we're unrealistically believing that we cannot make mistakes. Here, the focus ends up being on ourselves and self-punishment rather than the impact we've had on the other person. Of course, not feeling guilty isn't the same as making light of what happened. It's about accepting that we make mistakes and that we're not perfect. What we can do is to repair the damage we made, continue with our lives and learn for the future.

A final way in which guilt can be unhelpful is when we feel guilty about the emotions we experience. This often comes up in relation to anger. Many of us feel bad about feeling angry towards other people, especially if they're people we care for. We feel as if we're doing something wrong to them. However, we're not in control of what we feel. What we can control is how we behave in relation to our emotions. After all, feeling angry at someone is different to hurling abuse at them! Expecting that we shouldn't feel angry is unrealistic as we cannot control the fact that we feel angry unless we try to suppress the anger, which means that we still felt it in the first place! Again, the focus of guilt here is on punishing ourselves rather than on changing our behaviour which, in actual fact, might have been completely appropriate!

Shame

Shame is not about what we do but about how we judge ourselves. It runs deeper than guilt. When we feel ashamed, we see ourselves as intrinsically defective, unlovable and worthless beings – a waste of space. This triggers our fear of being rejected by others because of who we are. If we feel so worthless, we conclude that nobody would want us around. As a result, we can end up disconnecting from other people to avoid feeling the pain of rejection.

Shame comes in different forms and intensities. It can take the form of feeling ashamed, uncomfortable, shy, embarrassed, self-conscious, humiliated or degraded. It also manifests itself in our body language. We blush, look away or contract our body in such a way that we take up less space in an unintentional attempt to become invisible. We can find that we're labelling ourselves in disparaging ways, such as when we tell ourselves: "I'm such an idiot!" Shame also isolates us from others. It can make us hypersensitive to criticism and rejection or it can make us tolerate disrespect and abuse that is directed at us.

We start developing shame at a very early age. Unlike guilt, which we develop when we're about 3 to 6 years old, shame starts developing when we're just over a year old and start noticing other people's judgements about us. We're afraid that they will not love us if we're not good enough for them. We're afraid that if they see us for who we really are, they will react with disgust. We're afraid that they will say: "You should be ashamed of *yourself*!"

Shame is very much concerned with the prospect of feeling exposed to someone else as this would reinforce the feeling that we're someone to be ashamed of. However, in the process of fearing that an external person could judge us as being shameful, we end up internalising this shaming and judgemental regard and start seeing ourselves as unlovable and unworthy. Given that we can never escape our inner judging eye, we end up continuously labelling ourselves as shameful. This makes us feel trapped inside a self that we don't like. It makes us feel hopeless about ourselves. If we're only feeling guilt, we would be able to do something to make things right. But if *we* are what's wrong, then it feels like there's no hope of change!

Overcoming guilt and shame

Guilt needs forgiveness and letting go. It's about acknowledging what we did wrong, if that's the case. But it's also about letting go of the unrealistic notion that we can be perfect. We need to accept that we *will* make mistakes, that we *will* hurt others in life – both intentionally and unintentionally. Continuing to feel guilty will not change the past. We need to acknowledge our frail and imperfect selves and continue working towards living a better life.

Healing through shame is more difficult and painful because shame tries to remain hidden from our view. In order to work through shame, we need to expose that which we find disgusting or shameful in ourselves. The difficulty here lies with the fact that, the moment we start exposing our shame, this triggers more shame. We start feeling ashamed of feeling ashamed. So, we revert to hiding what's causing us to feel this added feeling of shame and, in so doing, render the shame invisible once again. But to disentangle ourselves from our shame, we need to continue exposing it. The best way to do so is to choose to be with people who are accepting and non-judgemental. By progressively exposing our shame, it starts loosening its grip on us and we learn to look at ourselves in a more positive light. But it's a process that feels utterly raw. It's pure vulnerability – and profoundly healing.

How to deal with shame and guilt

The following are some suggestions that can be helpful when dealing with both shame and unhelpful guilt.

- When you notice that you're experiencing shame or unhelpful guilt, recognise that what you're feeling is counter-productive to your growth.

- Try letting go of what you cannot control, such as unrealistic expectations or a perfectionist view of yourself.

These are some suggestions to better deal with guilt.

- Take responsibility for your behaviour. Take ownership of the wrong you did and don't shift your blame onto others.
- Understand the dynamic that might have pushed you to hurt someone else. Maybe you were very stressed or, as a child, you lived in violent surroundings and this pushes you to easily become aggressive. This process isn't about justifying your behaviour. It's about understanding what makes you act the way you do and that your wrong actions don't mean that you're a bad person.
- Ask for forgiveness from people you've hurt and acknowledge their anger or pain.
- Forgive yourself for what you did wrong.

Here are some suggestions to better deal with shame.

- Stop hiding the shame and instead start shedding light on it by changing your behaviours or talking about it with others.
- Identify whether shame is serving to mask another feeling, such as the fear of being yourself.
- Remind yourself that what you do is not the same as who you are.
- Recognise what triggers shame in you. Remind yourself that what you're feeling is a reaction and not who you really are.
- When you start feeling shame, connect to others instead of withdrawing. Reach out to friends and family with whom you feel safe. Meet new people. Don't let shame imprison you within yourself.
- Celebrate your inner strengths. Nobody is perfect, but nobody is rubbish. If you feel bad about yourself, find and celebrate the good parts of yourself.

The following exercises aim at helping you understand and shed light on your guilt and shame. They also offer you the possibility to work through some of your shame and unhelpful guilt.

How it relates to your life

How does this text relate to your life?
Write down anything that comes to mind, heart or body.

Exercises

01. Getting to know my shame

- ✍ Take some time to think about which aspect of yourself you feel most ashamed of. Picture that aspect clearly in your mind.
- ✍ While connecting to this feeling of shame, reflect on the following:
  - What does your shame feel like?
  - How does it manifest in your life at the moment?
  - How did it manifest before in your life?
  - If your shame was to express a judgement about you, what would it say? Imagine it as an external voice saying "You are … !"
- ✍ Write about the presence of shame in your life and how you feel that it judges you.

02. Drawing my shame and guilt

- ⤳ Think of something about you that makes you feel ashamed of yourself.
- ⤳ Connect to that feeling of shame.
- ⤳ In the first blank space below entitled 'My Shame', sketch a representation of your shame.

My Shame

- ∾ Now, think of something that you feel very guilty about.
- ∾ Connect to that feeling of guilt.
- ∾ In the blank space below entitled 'My Guilt', sketch a representation of your guilt.

My Guilt

- Look at both of your drawings. Observe any emotions or other reactions that come up for you.
- Write down what you've learnt about your shame and guilt in this exercise and what they bring up for you.

03. Shame and guilt in my body

- Stand or sit in front of a mirror and try looking straight into your eyes.

- Bring to mind something in yourself that makes you feel shame or guilt.

- Take a few deeper breaths while focusing on the shame or guilt. As much as possible, allow yourself to experience them in their fullness.

- Notice how your body reacts to the shame or guilt. Do you blush, avert your eyes or want to disappear? Is your spine upright or do you find yourself all hunched up?

- Now, allow your body to take a posture that represents how shame or guilt makes you feel. Stay in that posture for a while and notice what it feels like.

- After some time, check in with your body and emotions and see if you want to change anything in your posture to better reflect your feeling of shame or guilt.

- Write down what you learnt from this exercise about how shame or guilt manifest themselves in your body.

____

____

____

____

____

____

____

____

____

____

04. The posture of shame and guilt

- ✎ Observe how you normally sit or stand and think about the following questions:
    - Are you hunched or slumped?
    - Do you hold or cross your arms?
    - What is usually the expression on your face?
    - What is the usual volume of your voice?
    - Do you hold any tension in your body?
    - In what way does your body normally try to be smaller or closed in, rather than open and affirming?
- ✎ Now, imagine shame or guilt taking the form of a person. Imagine them adopting the same posture that you've just noted about yourself.
- ✎ Think about how it feels to see shame or guilt in that posture. What happens to your body as you imagine it? Do you shift your posture in any way?

❧ Write down your observations about how your posture reflects, and is reflected in, your shame or guilt.

05. Understanding my guilt

❧ Make a list of the main people that you feel you've hurt in your life, whether intentionally or unintentionally.

❧ Try to remember the conditions that led to you hurting them. An example could be having an argument with your partner and using your intimate knowledge of them against them.

- Think about why you didn't stop yourself from hurting them. What was driving you to hurt them? You might, for example, have been feeling very angry or you were feeling hurt and trapped. This isn't about excusing behaviour but about understanding the dynamics that led you to act in the way you did.

- Think of any additional conditions in your life that might have impacted how you acted in those situations. For example, if you were brought up in a family where your parents were constantly shouting abuse at each other or at you, you might have learnt that it's OK to lash out at one's partner when one is angry.

- Take some time to ponder over what you've just noted about yourself. In a gentle tone, tell yourself that you accept that you're human and that you can make mistakes and end up hurting others at times. You might find it hard to say this to yourself. If so, try imagining one of the closest people to you or someone you felt loved by in your past telling you this instead.

- Write down what came up for you in this exercise: the people you hurt, what led to that and how other aspects in your life impacted how you behaved in those situations. What does this teach you about the role of guilt in your life?

06. Messages I received from people close to me

- Think about people who you've felt close to in your life. This exercise isn't about blaming them but further understanding what you've learnt from them in relation to your worth as a person.

- Try to remember what kind of messages you received from them about yourself – about how lovable or worthy you are. Think about the following:

  - Did anyone ever imply or tell you that you're unlovable, undesirable or disgusting?

  - Did anybody ever threaten you with rejection, either physically or psychologically?

  - Did anyone ever tell you things like "I love you if you …" or "I don't love you if you …"?

  - As a child, if there were moments when you disobeyed or didn't do what was expected, were you told things like "You're making me sad!" or "You make me want to cry!"?

∾   Write down the names of these people and the messages you received in the table below.

Person	Messages I received

- Look at the list you just compiled and observe what emotions come up for you when you look at it.
- Take some time to think about how these messages could have affected the development of your shame or guilt.
- Write your reflections in the space below.

07. Messages I received from society

- Consider what messages you received from society, culture and the media about who the ideal person is when it comes to competence and success.
- Also bring to mind the people who were made fun of and criticised. What was said about being more of an extrovert or an introvert,

about being organised or disorganised, about being nerdy or cool, bright or stupid, active or lazy? What did people say about beautiful and ugly bodies and about how one should be living out one's sexual life?

❧ Now, observe if any of these negative messages also applied to you. How did that make you feel back then? And how does that make you feel nowadays? Is there a link between these messages and your experience of shame or guilt?

❧ Make a note of your memories and your reflections about this.

08. Opening up my body

- Look back at exercise 03 and adopt the position of shame or guilt that came up for you during that exercise.

- After some time, start making yourself physically bigger and more open. Straighten up and arch your back by looking upwards, moving your shoulders back and stretching out your arms upwards and backwards, as shown below.

- Regardless of whether you believe it or not, tell yourself out loud: "I'm great as I am!"

- Repeat the previous step, taking deeper breaths and increasing the volume of your voice.

- Stay in that open posture for a few minutes. Notice what emotions and thoughts come up. Take note of any tendency in your body to close up again.

- Write down what you learnt about how changing your posture impacts your feeling of shame or guilt.

____

____

____

____

____

____

____

____

____

____

____

____

____

____

09. Bringing warmth to shame and guilt

- ✍ Find a place where you won't be disturbed.

- ✍ Connect to your sense of shame or guilt. Notice where it's located in your body.

- ✍ Imagine that your hands are full of love and compassion.

- ✍ Place your hands on that part of your body where you sensed the shame or guilt. Feel the warmth of your hands and imagine it being a loving and compassionate presence that's touching and healing your shame or guilt.

- ∽ Notice how your body reacts to this. What happens to the area where you had located the shame or guilt? Maybe it wants to flinch away or it wants to be touched more. Does any other part of your body react to what's happening?

- ∽ Keep on doing this for as long as you like, enjoying the healing connection with yourself. Finally, express gratitude to yourself for having given yourself the time to be compassionate with your shame or guilt.

- ∽ In the space below, write down any reflections about what came up for you during the exercise.

10. Stepping out of shame and guilt

- Bring to mind an aspect of yourself that you feel ashamed of or something that you feel guilty about.

- Notice where and how you feel that shame or guilt in your body.

- Focus on that part of your body and feel it increasing in weight, noticing how it's weighing you down.

- Now, physically jump to the side imagining that you're leaving the weight of the shame or guilt behind you, right where you were standing.

- Take some time to notice how your body feels now. Do you feel physically freer and lighter now that you've stepped out of your shame and guilt?

- Observe your emotions and any thoughts that come to mind.

- Check if you're happy standing where you are or whether you want to take a further leap or two away from your shame or guilt. If so, take the leap and check again with how you're feeling.

- Write about your experience of leaving your shame behind. Does anything occur to you as to how you can apply this in everyday life?

11. Shifting posture

- Connect to your sense of shame or guilt and take the posture of shame or guilt that came up for you during exercise 04.

- Choose one aspect of your posture that you want to start changing. It can be deciding to keep your shoulders back, to keep your spine straight or to look forwards instead of looking down. Write this in the first column of the table below.

- During the coming week, focus only on this aspect of your posture. At various times during the day, check in with how you're positioning yourself and adjust your posture according to how you want to change it.

- After every time you shift your posture, bring your attention to how you're feeling.

- At the end of the week, check your posture again. Do you notice any kind of change? How does it feel to be more aware of your posture and be able to shift it? Write down your observations in the second column of the table below.

- Pick out another aspect of your posture that you want to change. Repeat this exercise as often as you need.

An aspect of my posture that I want to change this week	Changes I observe after a week

Aspect of my posture	Changes I observe

12. Facing those who make me feel ashamed or guilty

- Bring to mind someone who elicits feelings of shame or guilt in you.

- Imagine you're in front of that person and notice your physical reaction. Do you flush, look away, want to become invisible, make yourself smaller or blame and criticise yourself?

- Now, engage in an action that counteracts that automatic physical reaction you just experienced. If your face flushed, take a deep breath or sigh. If you looked away, look at other things in the room in a purposeful way or even look directly at that person. If you wanted to become invisible, imagine the other person fading away. If you made yourself smaller, lengthen your spine and straighten up. If you blamed or criticised yourself, place your hand on your heart and imagine sending loving warmth to yourself.

- Notice what kind of impact this has on your feeling of shame or guilt.
- Write down what you learnt about your bodily reactions to shame or guilt and about what you can do to counteract those feelings the next time you meet the person concerned.

13. A compassionate voice

- Think of one shameful or guilty thing that you did.
- Use the space below to write it down in all its detail.

- Make an audio recording of yourself while reading it aloud.
- Now, imagine yourself as a very loving and compassionate person. Maybe you know someone like that and want to imagine that you're them instead.
- Play back the recording you just made. What do you feel when you listen to the recording? What do you feel towards the person who's telling you about this shameful or guilty thing they did?
- Think of what you would want to tell them and write your response down in the space below.

- Now, make another audio recording, this time reading the response of this compassionate person aloud.

- Every time you feel shame or guilt, listen to the recording of the loving and compassionate voice while noticing your emotional and bodily reactions to it.

14. If I had no guilt

- List three to five things you still feel guilty about having done in your life.
- For each one of them, imagine what would happen if you suddenly were to stop feeling any guilt about the situation.
- Notice what thoughts, emotions or body sensations come up for you and note them down in the table below.

What I still feel guilty about	What would happen if I suddenly stop feeling any guilt	Thoughts, emotions or body sensations that come up

<table>
<tr><td></td><td></td><td></td></tr>
<tr><td></td><td></td><td></td></tr>
</table>

15. Let the guilt fly away

- ❧ Take a piece of paper and make a list of the things you feel guilty about.

- ❧ Burn the paper, bury it underground or find another symbolic way of destroying it. While doing so, imagine that you're letting go of the guilt and that you're being forgiven for what you did.

- ❧ Write about your experience of engaging in this exercise.

16. Dancing out my freedom

- Imagine that you're completely free from all unhelpful guilt and shame.

- Observe who you would be, what you would look like, how you would sit and stand and how you would speak. Think of how you would behave in different areas of your life and how you would relate to others.

- Stay with this image in your mind for a while, using your breathing to connect to it and allowing it to become more real.

- Notice how it feels emotionally and in your body to have this kind of freedom.

- Now, dance out your freedom. Don't worry about how and which parts of your body you're moving. Just dance out the freedom in an unhindered way. Maybe you want to shout or scream or you want to sing as you dance. Do it! Enjoy the feeling of freedom. Feel free to put on any music that helps you express this sense of freedom.

- After you stop, take some time to notice how you feel and any lingering physical sensations.

> Write about your experience of using your body to give yourself freedom from guilt.

17. Asking for forgiveness

> Look at the list in exercise 05 where you wrote down the names of some people you've hurt.

> Pick three people from that list and consciously decide to ask them for forgiveness.

> If possible, find a suitable time to meet up with them and ask them for forgiveness. When doing so, make sure of the following:

- Admit that you hurt them. Own up to your actions and don't make excuses.
- Recognise that they have a right to be angry at you and that they can express their anger towards you.
- Do not accept abuse. This is about forgiveness, not disrespect.

∽ After you meet each person, take some time to reflect upon your experience and how it felt to ask for forgiveness. Did anything unexpected come out of the encounter? Write down your observations below.

∽ If you cannot meet the person face-to-face, you can write a letter and send it to them or find a place where you can read it aloud, imagining that they're standing in front of you. You can still use the space below to note down your reflections on your experience.

Person I've hurt	How it felt to ask for forgiveness	Any other reflections about the encounter

18. Exposing shame

- Think of someone you really trust and whom you can physically meet up with.

- Bring to mind one thing that you would like to do or say that goes against one aspect of shame about yourself that you experience. It could be something about your life in the present, a story about your past or desires that you have for your future. It could be singing a song or showing a part of your body that you feel ashamed of.

- Meet the other person and clearly express how important this is for you.

- Ask them not to comment, analyse or judge what you're doing or saying. Instead, ask them to simply listen or watch, to bear witness to you stepping out of your shame.

- In the end, ask them to share with you how they felt about having the opportunity to witness you revealing this part of yourself. This is about their emotions, not their evaluation.

- Finally, share with them how you felt about having the chance to overcome some shame in their presence.

- Maybe you want to end the moment by giving each other a really warm and long hug!

- Afterwards, find a comfortable space alone where you can reflect upon the experience.

- Write down what it felt like for you and what you learnt about the impact of exposing your own shame in the presence of a safe person.

~ 10 ~

ON THE INNER CRITICAL VOICE

Have you ever talked negatively to yourself? Maybe you said things like "I'm such an idiot!", "I never get it right!" or "What's the point in even trying?" Or have you ever imagined that other people were thinking negative things about you and you said to yourself things like "They don't appreciate me!" or "They're too good for me!"

Maybe you only do this occasionally or maybe you do it often. Regardless of how often you do it and how intensely you engage in this negative self-talk, it's always one that makes you feel bad about yourself because it criticises you and puts you down.

At times, it can be beneficial to have a constructive, critical approach to ourselves. It pushes us to improve ourselves and our situation. In doing so, it enables us to grow rather than leaving us stuck in a mediocre way of living.

Audio files for this chapter can be accessed at
thehorsesmouth.michaelconti.net/lbwy-ch10
or by scanning the adjacent QR code.

However, this critical approach can easily switch to a negative inner critical voice. We're not talking about an actual voice, as would be the case when one is hallucinating. Instead, we're referring to a set of negative thoughts, beliefs and attitudes that degrade, judge and punish us. The inner critical voice is an aspect of ourselves that's turned against us. Not only does this inner voice criticise what we do, but it also targets who we are by concluding that we're not good enough, that we're lacking in some way, that we're unlovable and unlikeable and that we'll never be otherwise. The critical voice can also transform itself into a negative attitude towards others. This leads us to view the world in a pessimistic way and, in the process, isolates us from those around us.

The intensity of the inner critical voice can vary. It often takes the form of a mild self-reproach, such as when we tell ourselves: "I should have known better!" However, it can also take the form of very strong self-accusations. This leads us to believe that we're hopelessly incompetent and unworthy.

A negative critical voice can heavily impact our well-being. It can strongly deplete our self-esteem. This can end up confirming the belief that we're not good enough which, in turn, further strengthens the critical voice. It can lead us to experience depression, anxiety, stress or other mental health conditions. When the negative critical voice is very prominent, it can lead to self-harming behaviours, such as addiction or self-inflicted physical harm. It also strongly affects our relationships, such as when we keep ourselves in an abusive relationship because, deep down, we believe that we're not really worthy of being loved.

How we develop the inner critical voice

The negative thoughts and beliefs about ourselves and others develop primarily during the first part of life. Perhaps our parents or caregivers constantly pushed us to do better, to achieve more, to excel. They probably had our best interests in mind, but we ended up learning that, in order to gain their approval and love, we need to satisfy their expectations. Or we might have had parents, caregivers or teachers who criticised us on a regular basis, clearly showing us that we're not good enough as we are.

Another way in which we develop a negative critical voice is when we're confronted with hurtful experiences in our families while we're still young. An example of this is domestic violence. Such situations can lead us to try to improve the situation. However, given that we're still too young, this isn't possible and so we experience a strong sense of failure. We might even blame ourselves for what's happening. This is because children usually assume that caregivers love them even when they're being abusive towards them. Consequently, they conclude that they're to blame for anything bad that happens as it 'can't' be the caregiver's fault. They conclude that they themselves are bad and unlovable. Such experiences can lead us to develop a negative belief about ourselves that then forms the basis of the inner critical voice.

When we become adults

Although unpleasant and actually harmful, this critical voice was probably useful when we were young. It kept us safe and offered us security. By being critical of ourselves, we increased the chance of winning the love of the adults around us. By seeing ourselves as unworthy of love, we reduced the pain we felt when adults treated us badly because we believed that it was our fault that they were acting the way they did. As a result, we learnt that, in order to be safe and loved, we need to obey the inner critical voice.

The problem is that this negative voice accompanies us into adulthood and blocks us from developing new ways of responding to novel situations. Our reactions remain stuck in our past, mirroring yesterday's reality rather than the one we're living today. In other words, although the critical voice might have served a purpose in our past, it's now obsolete and no longer useful – but we know no other way.

How can we change our inner critical voice?

Changing our inner critical voice is not an easy task. Ultimately, it's a voice that wants to protect us. Consequently, the moment we try to change it, it will resist us as it believes it's crucial for our security. Approaching it aggressively will only reinforce the feeling of needing it. Instead, we need to approach it gently and compassionately. However, we also need to approach it firmly because, otherwise, it will never lose its hold on us. The following are some ways that can help you start changing the impact that the inner critical voice has on you.

- Identify in which areas of your life you're highly critical of yourself. Observe how you criticise yourself and summarise it in a single sentence.

- When you find yourself feeling negative, check whether you've just been criticising yourself. The critical voice often functions at an unconscious level and so we frequently only notice it through its effect on our emotions.

- Visualise the critical voice as someone or something outside of you. Give it a name. Separate it from your viewpoint as this helps you reframe yourself in a more realistic light.

- Whenever you criticise yourself, bring to mind the externalised critical voice that you imagined. Instead of using statements in the form "I am …", imagine that it's the critical voice that's talking to you and so articulate the criticism using "You are …" statements.

- Start constructing an inner positive and encouraging voice. Imagine people you know who care for you speaking to you about yourself. Imagine their voice in your head in order to counteract the critical voice.

- Capture any positive feedback you receive in a small journal and carry it around with you. Read through some of the pages when you find that you're criticising yourself.

- When you notice that you're criticising yourself, give yourself a hug. If you're not in a situation where you can do it freely, try crossing your arms and giving yourself a gentle squeeze instead. Allow yourself to feel being loved in a physical way, something that can help drown out the negative voice. The more the critical voice makes itself heard, the more affection you need to show yourself!

The following exercises aim at helping you become more aware of your inner critical voice. They help you understand it better and find ways to diminish its impact on you while, at the same time, developing a more positive approach to yourself.

How it relates to your life

How does this text relate to your life?
Write down anything that comes to mind, heart or body.

Exercises

01. Observing my critical voice

- ✍ Take note of when you say negative things to, or about, yourself. Notice how often you say that, how it makes you feel emotionally and what physical sensations accompany it.
- ✍ Write down these statements and your observations in the table below.
- ✍ For each one of the statements, check whether they remind you of anyone having said or implied something similar about you.

Negative statement	Observations, emotions and body sensations	Whom it reminds me of

02. My critical voice on paper

In the blank space below draw your inner critical voice. Don't allow it to stop you from giving yourself the freedom to draw it in any way you want to.

My Inner Critical Voice

Look back at the drawing. What do you notice about it? What does this show you about yourself? Write down your observations below.

03. How old it makes me feel

- Bring to mind your critical voice. When you hear it speak to you, take note of how old it makes you feel. Do you feel that you're still an adult or does it make you feel like a child?

- If the critical voice makes you feel as if you were a child, how old would that child be? Do you have any memories of how you perceived yourself, how you were judged by others or how good or bad things were for you at that time of your life?

- In the space below, write down what came up for you in this exercise and any memories that came to mind.

04. My memories of being criticised

- The next time you catch yourself criticising yourself, try to recall if there was anyone who used to tell you similar things when you were young or if you used to say such things to yourself. What are your earliest memories of these?

- Do you notice any connection between your past experience of criticism and your inner critical voice today?

- Write down your observations and what you learnt in the space below.

05. How I feel towards those who criticised me

◈ Bring to mind people who were critical towards you in your past. List their names down in the table below.

◈ Recall in which ways they were critical of you and notice any emotions you feel towards them as you do so. Bear in mind that you might find it difficult to do this if you've been criticised by people you love. This is because we often struggle to accept that we can also experience feelings of anger, disappointment or hate towards people we love. So, try to let yourself feel the emotions you're feeling without judging them because they might not be the only emotions that you feel towards that person.

◈ Write down your emotions below, next to the person's name.

Person's name	Emotions

∽ Now, look back at what you've written. Is there any thought, memory, emotion or body sensation that comes up for you? In the space below, take note of this and what came up for you during this exercise.

06. A three-way conversation with the critical voice

∽ Set up three chairs in a circle.

∽ Sit on one of the chairs. When you're sitting on this chair, you are yourself. On one of the other chairs is sitting your inner critical voice. On the other chair is sitting a nurturing and caring voice. Notice how it feels for you to have these two voices sitting on the chairs next to you. Do you notice any particular physical sensations?

∽ Now, sit on the chair where there's the critical voice. When you sit down, imagine that you've left yourself behind in the first chair and that you've now solely become your critical voice. Notice what it feels like to be in that chair and how you feel towards the other two chairs. Get in touch with what you want to say as the critical voice. Now, allow yourself the freedom to speak it aloud while addressing your words to the other chairs. What would you say and to which of those chairs?

❧ When you're done, go and sit in the chair where there's the nurturing voice. Imagine that you're a positive voice that's nurturing, gentle, encouraging and caring. Give yourself some time to embody this new side of yourself. How does it feel? Is there anything you want to say to the critical voice that has just spoken? Is there anything that you would like to say to the chair where you were sitting down initially? Let yourself speak freely.

❧ Finally, come back to the first chair you were sitting on. Notice how you feel after having heard both voices speak. Notice any particular physical sensations that come up. Is there anything that you would like to say back to either of them? Give yourself the freedom to speak aloud to either of those chairs.

❧ If you feel that any of the other voices would like to add to, or comment on, what you're saying, go sit in that chair and speak from that side of yourself.

❧ Always finish the exercise as yourself.

❧ In the end, imagine that the two voices leave their respective chairs and that you're left alone. How did it feel to be sitting in those chairs? What has stayed with you from the conversation that you've just had? Is there anything that the positive voice said that can help you better handle your inner critical voice?

❧ In the space below, write down what you learnt about yourself and how you can better handle the critical voice.

07. Visualising the inner critical voice

- Find a place where you won't be disturbed and assume a comfortable position.

- Imagine that your critical voice is no longer inside you but is there, in front of you. Notice what posture it assumes. Observe what it looks like, how it speaks and how it's looking at you.

- While doing this, check in with your breathing and emotions. Do you notice any change?

- Now, imagine that this critical voice is shrinking in size. Observe it getting smaller and smaller until it disappears.

- ⌇ Give yourself some time to be present with yourself without having this critical voice around. How does it feel? What happens to your breathing and emotions when you're alone without this voice?
- ⌇ In the space below, write about how your emotions and breathing are impacted by the critical voice.

08. Turning the volume knobs

- The next time you hear the inner critical voice putting you down, imagine that you have a large volume knob in front of you.

- Imagine yourself starting to turn the volume down by turning the knob. Imagine the volume of the negative voice decreasing until you can't hear it anymore.

- If you have any positive voice inside you, imagine using another volume knob to turn its volume up until it's deafening!

09. Telling it to go away

- Go to a place where you can make as much noise as you want to, such as a beach, a park or a very busy main road.

- Imagine that the inner critical voice is standing right in front of you.

- Connect with how you feel when you picture it there, looking at you. In particular, connect to any feeling of anger or frustration that you might be feeling.

- Now, think of what you want to tell that voice for it to leave you in peace. You might say something like "Go away!" or "Leave me alone!" You can use any kind of language you want that allows you to express yourself fully. And say it out loud.

- Take a deep breath and repeat what you just said but this time increasing the volume. Continue repeating this, each time taking a deep breath and increasing the volume.

- Only stop when you feel quite depleted of energy or when you don't feel the need to continue.

- Notice how your body feels after having done this. What are the emotions and thoughts that came up during and after the exercise?

- Write down your reflections in the space below.

____

____

____

____

____

____

____

____

____

____

____

____

____

10. Taking power in front of the critical voice

- ல Find a place where you won't be disturbed. Imagine that the inner voice is criticising you.

- ல Connect with how this makes you feel and allow yourself to adopt a position with your body that reflects this emotion. Continue shifting your posture until it's in line with how that critical voice makes you feel.

- ல Stay for a while in that position. Notice any memories, emotions or body sensations that come up for you.

- ல Notice if there's any desire to take any action in relation to how you're positioned or in relation to the critical voice.

- Now, focus on your breathing. Feel your breath as it goes deep into your belly, your abdomen, your core. Imagine that this is a place of inner power that's strong enough to overcome the critical voice.

- While remaining connected to your place of power in your core, start opening up your posture and standing up tall, imagining that the critical voice is getting smaller and smaller.

- Stand up with your arms outstretched, occupying the biggest amount of space possible. Open your face out wide. Feel yourself getting larger as the critical voice continues getting smaller.

- Give yourself permission to make any sound that makes you feel powerful or to say anything you want to that critical voice. You might want to shout or scream at it. Let yourself unleash your power in front of its oppressive force! And all the time connect to your inner sense of power.

- Finally, come to a standstill and allow yourself to breathe normally. Scan your body and observe any sensations you have. Check in with your emotions. What does it feel like to have given yourself physical power over the inner critical voice?

- Use the space below to write about your experience during this exercise. Is there any image that you can come back to in moments when the critical voice rears its head again?

11. Rewarding myself

- Make a list of a few simple things that you really enjoy and that don't cost a lot of money.

- Every time you notice your negative voice criticising you, tell yourself that, instead of following that voice, you will take care of yourself and reward yourself with one of the things you have on your list. In this way, you turn every moment of self-criticism into a moment of self-love.

List of simple things I will use as rewards

12. "I'm good enough!"

- Print out in large letters the text "I'm good enough!" or something similar that's the opposite of how the negative voice makes you feel about yourself.

- Put it up in prominent places in your house or at your workplace and every time you look at it, say it aloud to yourself!

13. Developing a positive script

- Take some time to think about someone who's nurturing towards you. What would they say to you in order to counteract what your critical voice tells you? It can be a friend, a family member or someone fictitious, but it needs to be someone who has your best interests at heart.

- In the space below, write down what you think they would say even if you don't believe it.

- Make an audio recording of yourself reading this. Listen to it at least at the beginning and end of each day and especially in moments when you notice that your inner voice is criticising you.

- After you've done this for a couple of weeks, start saying aloud the same thing to yourself every time you criticise yourself. Keep doing this until you feel that this positive voice has become more part of you.

14. A letter to the critical voice

- The critical voice is usually trying to protect you or is the remnant of past experiences where you were actually hurt. Write a letter to it where you show your understanding of why it's there and what it's trying to achieve.

- After you've expressed your understanding, write about how it's affecting you and what you need it to do, or stop doing, in order for you to enjoy a better life.

- Finally, record yourself reading this letter out and listen to the recording several times during the week so that you develop an inner voice that answers back to the criticisms of the negative voice.

- Use the space below or any other sheet of paper to write your letter. Feel free to add any other things that you learnt from this exercise.

15. Breathing in compassion and warmth

- When you notice the inner critical voice talking to you, take a moment to focus on your breathing and take some deeper breaths that reach deep down into your abdomen.

- Imagine that, every time you inhale, you're breathing in compassion and warmth that pushes away and melts away the harsh criticism of your negative voice. Imagine it happening in gentle waves, one after the other.

∽ In the end, scan your emotions and your body, noticing any sensations that are present for you. Repeat this exercise until you notice that you're in a more positive place than when you started.

∽ Write down what your experience during this exercise was and how you can apply it in your everyday life.

~ 11 ~

ON 'SHOULD' STATEMENTS

We all have our beliefs about what is right or wrong. We all have our principles and set of morals. And we all have a list of what we ought to do, or not. These things are important when it comes to living with others. They stop us from pursuing our desires at the expense of the group we belong to.

However, if this set of rules is based on our expectations rather than our actual needs, it can have a negative impact on us. In this case, we develop a set of 'should' statements based on our expectations and beliefs and these statements determine what we should and shouldn't do. 'Should' statements aren't just a desire. They're accompanied by a strong sense of *having* to do something, that someone else *should* act in a particular way or that circumstances *ought* to be different. So, we end up thinking or saying things like "I should look slimmer!", "I should not be wasting time!", "They should not be angry at me!" or "They should have sent a thank you card!"

Audio files for this chapter can be accessed at **thehorsesmouth.michaelconti.net/lbwy-ch11** *or by scanning the adjacent QR code.*

At face value, 'should' statements can appear to be very sensible. However, the problem with them is that they're inflexible and leave no room for negotiation. They make it feel as if nothing else matters. They end up controlling our behaviours and emotions. If we don't manage to live up to them, we feel hopeless or that we're a failure. And when we uphold them, we feel a sense of righteousness.

'Should' statements aim more at satisfying an expectation than actually dealing with reality. Although the expectations can seem realistic, they're actually the result of black-and-white thinking. Rather than helping us improve our reality, 'should' statements are a form of criticism towards ourselves, others or life situations. They disconnect us from our desires and prevent us from being ourselves in a freer way.

How we develop 'should' statements

We develop our 'should' statements throughout our whole life, right from the moment when we're born. We absorb them from the people around us: parents, siblings, caregivers, friends, teachers, employers, colleagues and the media. Sometimes they're directly taught to us, like when we're criticised or reprimanded. 'Should' statements that we learn at a young age have a particularly strong impact on the way we deal with expectations later on in life. As a child, we might have been told that we should be quiet, obedient, polite, neat, contain ourselves and that we shouldn't cry or make a mess. We might have been taught 'appropriate' ways of interacting with our body, which parts we can touch or not and in which circumstances. And we also end up learning that this is what's expected of us to get approval from others.

In the process of learning these expectations, we internalise them. We make them our own and start believing them. We end up policing ourselves and dictating to ourselves how we should be and act. If we step away from these expectations, we feel guilty and ashamed and might even feel hatred towards ourselves.

As a result of these 'should' statements, we disconnect from our desires. We lose touch with our genuine self and instead impose a way of being that satisfies the expectations of others. This can lead to living a more restricted life and can result in anxiety, depression or physical tension. It can also generate a lot of suppressed anger that erupts at different points in our life without us knowing where it came from.

Freeing ourselves from 'should' statements

It takes a lot of practice to stop being controlled by our 'should' statements. The following are some ways that can help you start freeing yourself from their tyranny.

- When you find yourself thinking in the form of a 'should' statement, ask yourself: Is it really true or is it just a statement I've internalised as I was growing up? Who says that things should be so? Where is it written? Is this helping me grow and making me happier, or not?

- When you notice you're thinking in terms of a 'should' statement, change it to a statement about preference. For example, instead of saying "I should go to the gym four times a week!", say, "My goal is to go to the gym four times a week."

- When you feel that someone has done something that they *shouldn't* be doing, ask yourself: Why shouldn't they? What does it say about my expectations?

- Do not compare yourself to others. It only creates unrealistic expectations.

- Get to know yourself better. Distinguish between who you are and who you would like to be. Learn to accept the genuine you rather than the ideal you.

- Make sure that, at some point during each day, you fit in something that you *want* to do rather than that you *have* to do.

- Every time you notice that you've stepped away from your usual 'should' statements, reward yourself. The more times you do it, the more rewards you'll receive!

- Be gentle with yourself when you find that you're thinking in terms of 'should' statements. Don't fall into the trap of telling yourself: "I *shouldn't* follow 'should' statements!"

The exercises that follow aim at helping you become more aware of your 'should' statements, understand them more and find ways of freeing yourself from them.

How it relates to your life

How does this text relate to your life?
Write down anything that comes to mind, heart or body.

Exercises

01. Listing my 'should' statements

- ✎ Use the table below to make a list of all the 'should' statements that apply to you. They can be big statements, like "I *should* be a good person!", or simpler ones, like "I *should* wake up early to make better use of my morning!"

- ✎ Go through the list and score each one according to how important and strong they are for you, using a scale of 1 (least) to 10 (most).

- ✎ After you've listed your 'should' statements, go through the list and think of what might be the worst consequence should you not follow each statement. Write this in the box next to it.

'Should' statement	Scale of importance (1 – 10)	Consequence of not following the 'should' statement

'Should' statement	Scale	Consequence

02. Whom I experience 'should' statements with the most

∽   Take some time to think about the people with whom you experience more 'should' statements. Is it with your parents, your partner or your children? Is it with your colleagues, employees or your boss? Is it with anybody else?

∽   Make a list of these people in the table below. Use a scale of 1 (least) to 10 (most) and note down how strongly you experience these 'should' statements with each one of them.

Person	Strength of 'should' statement (1-10)

03. "You should!"

- Stand in front of a mirror. Stretch your arm forwards and point your finger at your image in the mirror.

- Look at the list you compiled in exercise 01. Using a stern and strong voice, say one of those statements out loud in the form: "You should [what you wrote in your statement] !"

- Try to maintain eye contact with yourself as you say that statement.

- Notice how your body reacts when you hear that statement or if you want to reply in any way. Try to allow yourself to react freely.

- Notice any emotions that come up.

- Now, drop your arms to your sides and close your eyes. Take a couple of calming breaths. You might want to use square breathing or 4-7-8 breathing as described in chapter 02 (p. 9).

- Repeat this exercise with other 'should' statements on your list.

- Write down your observations about the reactions you experienced during this exercise. What did you learn about yourself?

04. Free from my 'should' statements

- Find a place where you can be relaxed, preferably lying down.

- Go back to the list of 'should' statements you wrote in exercise 01.

- Pick one of the statements that has a low score and imagine yourself being completely free from having to follow it.

- Notice what emotions and thoughts come up as you imagine yourself being free from it. Notice any body reactions you get or any desire to change your posture and, if so, move accordingly.

- After some time, go back to the list and select statements that you rated with a higher score. Continue repeating this exercise until you reach the statements that have the highest score.

- In the space below, write down what you learnt about the experience of imagining yourself to be free from your 'should' statements. Notice what happened in your emotions, thoughts and body sensations or movements.

05. The early voice of 'should'

- ◈ Go back to your list of 'should' statements in exercise 01.

- ◈ Imagine each one being said to you in the form: "You should [what you wrote in your statement] !"

- ◈ Whose voice do you mostly hear telling you these things? Try being as honest as possible with yourself. This isn't about blaming others but about recognising who had a strong influence on the 'should' statements that you carry around with you today.

- ◈ Write down your reflections about this exercise in the space below.

06. How I learnt my 'should' statements

- Take some time to reflect on how you learnt how you *should* be. Was it through punishment, through love being withheld or any other way? What used to happen when you weren't who you were expected to be?

- In the space below, write down your observations and how you think this affected the development of your 'should' statements.

07. Drawing my 'should' voice

- In the space below, draw the voice that tells you: "You *should!*"
- Now, draw yourself in the same space with this voice.

"You should!"

"You should!"

∛ Take a good look at the image. In the space below, write down what strikes you about what you drew. What does it tell you about how you position yourself in relation to your 'should' statements?

08. A timeline of my 'should' statements

∛ The horizontal line below represents your life. Use the space above and below this line to sketch another line that represents how strongly you followed, or rebelled against, your 'should' statements throughout your life. The further up you go on the graph, the more you followed the 'should' statements. The further down you go, the more you opposed them.

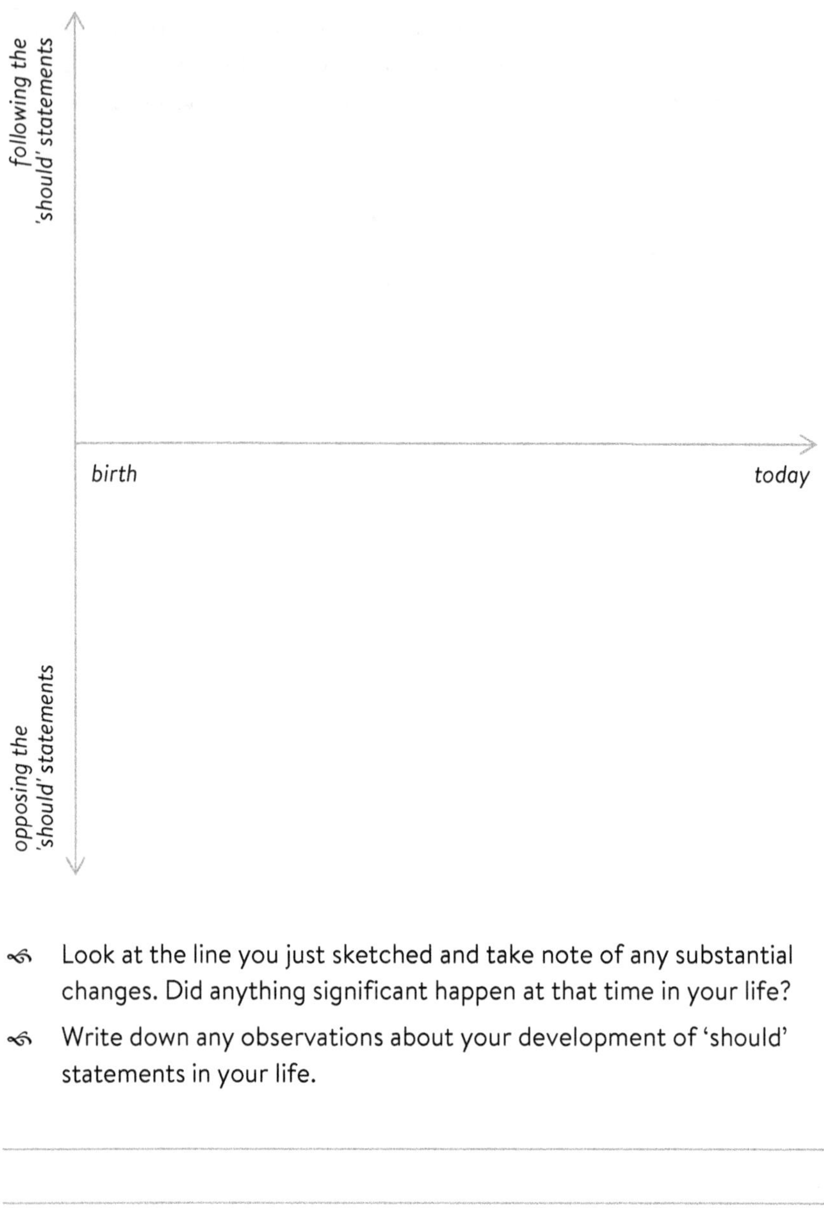

- Look at the line you just sketched and take note of any substantial changes. Did anything significant happen at that time in your life?
- Write down any observations about your development of 'should' statements in your life.

09. Facing those who taught me my 'should' statements

- From exercise 02, pick one of the people with whom you experienced the most 'should' statements with.

- Stay in a standing position during this exercise. If this isn't comfortable for you, sit up as straight as possible.

- Take a few minutes to imagine this person standing in front of you. How old do they make you feel? Do you feel like an adult with them or do they make you feel as if you were a child? Notice what emotions come up in relation to them.

- Imagine you had all the freedom possible. What do you feel like saying to that person? Say this aloud while you imagine them standing in front of you.
- Repeat this with other people on your list.
- Write about your experience of facing those who taught you the 'should' statements and of facing them as the person you are today.

10. "I will not!"

- Look at the statements in exercise 01.

- Stand in front of a mirror and point at your image in the mirror. While maintaining eye contact with your reflection, use a stern and strong voice to say out loud one of those statements in the form: "You should [what you wrote in your statement] !"

- Now, place your arms on your hips and stand up tall and proud.

- Take a deep breath and, using a clear and strong voice, state out loud: "I will not!" or "No!"

- With the next couple of breaths, check what that felt like.

- Repeat what you just said in a more forceful way. You can increase your volume, use another language or use gestures that make it look like you're pushing away the 'should' statement. It can also be helpful to exhale forcefully as you push it away.

- Repeat this as often as necessary until you feel more empowered in front of that 'should' statement.

- You can repeat this exercise with other 'should' statements.

- In the space below, write about what it felt like to be able to say "No!" to your 'should' statement. Take note of what thoughts, emotions and body sensations came up for you.

____

____

____

____

____

____

____

____

____

____

____

____

____

____

____

____

11. Being different for a week

- Go back to the list of 'should' statements in exercise 01.

- Pick a 'should' statement that has one of the lowest scores and make a decision not to obey it during the coming week.

- Every time you succeed in ignoring it, note what the situation was, what you felt the moment you thought of the 'should' statement, how you acted differently, what you felt afterwards and what the consequence of acting differently was. Write these down below.

Situation	Immediate feeling or sensation	Alternative action	Feeling or sensation afterwards	Consequence
e.g. I felt that I should pay for drinks when meeting a friend.	*Felt like something was crushing me and a knot in my stomach.*	*I told the cashier that we're splitting the bill.*	*Felt light in my stomach and could breathe more freely.*	*We are still friends as we ever were before!*

Situation	Immediate feeling or sensation	Alternative action	Feeling or sensation afterwards	Consequence

- ∽ At the end of the week, look back at the table. What do you notice about your behaviour? What were the consequences of not obeying the 'should' statement?
- ∽ Repeat this exercise with other 'should' statements that you have.
- ∽ Write down what you've learnt about the actual consequences of not obeying one of the 'should' statements.

12. An affirming letter

- Imagine yourself as being your greatest and closest friend.
- In the space below, write a letter to yourself, encouraging yourself to act in the opposite way to the 'should' statements that stifle you.

- ✍ Make an audio recording of yourself while reading the letter aloud.
- ✍ Play the recording to yourself. Notice what happens to your emotions and body sensations while you listen to it.
- ✍ Every time you catch yourself following your 'should' statements, play back this recording to yourself.

13. I am free to …

- ✍ Think of how you would want to live as a freer person. What desires or aspects of your character would you change? How would you act differently?
- ✍ Turn each thing that comes up into a statement that affirms that you're free to be so even though it doesn't feel true at the moment.
- ✍ Write down the statements in the space below.

I'm free to
I'm free to
I'm free to
I'm free to
I'm free to
I'm free to
I'm free to
I'm free to
I'm free to
I'm free to
I'm free to

- Now, choose one of the statements. Write it on a piece of paper and put it up in your room or in a place you spend a lot of time in. Refer to this paper as often as possible, imaging that the affirming statement is true. Notice any emotions, thoughts or body sensations that come up for you when you do so.
- As days go by, observe if you notice any difference in how you feel or in your behaviour.
- Repeat this with other statements.
- Write down how it feels to be telling yourself affirming statements and any changes that you see in yourself in the process.

12

ON CONTROL

How do you feel about being organised and structured? How do you feel about letting go of structure and going with the flow? Some of us tend more towards one, others more towards the other. Some of us need to have a higher level of control in life. We want to make sure that things are in place and that we've planned for unforeseen circumstances. On the other hand, others feel inhibited by structure. They prefer to flow with what comes along. And the majority of us lie somewhere in between these two ends of the spectrum.

Being in control

If we like being in control, we probably also like structure. Structure offers us security. We probably also tend to be more task-oriented and

Audio files for this chapter can be accessed at **thehorsesmouth.michaelconti.net/lbwy-ch12** *or by scanning the adjacent QR code.*

rational in our approach to life, as these make it easier to achieve our desired outcomes.

Being in control can make us feel like we're indispensable to those around us. It puts us in a position where our ability to keep things under control enables the world around us to function. This provides a purpose for our need for control and makes it even harder to shift our perspective. We might think that we "*have* to clean the dishes tonight!" or that we "*have* to write that email tomorrow!", as if not doing so will have disastrous consequences.

Although it's helpful to have some degree of control in life, a strong focus on control also comes with its downside. It can lead to emotional disturbance, such as depression, anxiety or a very short temper. The energy required to keep things under control can lead to addictive behaviours so as to ease the internal pressure. Trying to be in control can negatively impact our relationships as partners feel that we're trying to control them and friends feel that we're too demanding and critical. Having controlling parents can lead to outbursts of rage or mental health difficulties, both when we're still young and later on in life.

Seeking to control our surroundings

Our desire to be in control often results from our fear of being at the mercy of someone or something else. When we don't feel in control, we feel more exposed to something dangerous potentially happening to us. To avoid this, we try to control the environment and people around us. We plan for specific outcomes and we get attached to them. And because of the sense of security that this offers us, we try to achieve them at all costs. Any alternative becomes a risk we're ready to take a long way to avoid.

The desire for control can also be motivated by low self-esteem. By reaching the specific outcomes we fixate ourselves on, we feel less insecure about ourselves. And to ensure that we reach those outcomes, we need to be more in control. Similarly, we might strive for control in order to feel powerful as this makes us feel more secure about ourselves. But underneath all this lies our low self-worth.

Seeking to control our emotions

While some of us try to feel secure by controlling our external environment, others try to control themselves and, in particular, their emotions. By trying to control our emotions, we believe that we can decrease the likelihood of feeling overwhelmed. We can also try doing this by attempting to control our thinking as our thoughts will trigger emotions. For example, in trying to control our aggressive thoughts, we're ultimately trying to control our feeling of anger. And if we try to control our obsessive thinking about the quality of our work, what we're actually trying to control is our fear of failing or not being good enough.

Wanting to control our emotions can also be a result of having experienced trauma. In this case, the emotions we experience can be overwhelmingly strong and debilitating so we try to find ways to block them. We become highly controlling, such that we end up preventing ourselves from manifesting emotions in the first place. We become cold and 'emotionless'.

Yet another reason why we might try to control our emotions is because of our upbringing or cultural norms. Some families look down upon certain forms of emotional expression. Parents often tell children to "Tone it down!" and to "Be quiet!" Boys are often told not to cry or to "man up". Expressions of frustration or anger are often met with frowns and reprimands. In some cultures, emotional expression is seen as a weakness, especially in the case of men. These constraints that are placed on emotions teach us that we ought to control them. Consequently, we learn to suppress those emotions and to remove them from our awareness because we believe that, if we don't see them, they don't exist.

Being unstructured

The opposite of being in control involves living life in a structureless manner. We go with the flow with no particular consideration of the consequences of our decisions. As a result, we end up making very short-sighted and impulsive decisions. When we're predominantly spontaneous or free from structure, we tend to be very emotional and to express ourselves very bluntly.

There are numerous reasons why we value being free from structure so highly. We might have been in situations where we weren't set any boundaries when we were young – we were allowed to do whatever we wanted, whenever we wanted. Maybe our parents were usually away, didn't care or thought that this is a better way of life. But being brought up without boundaries teaches us that life is limitless, an illusion that's still hard to let go of even when we miss that flight we arrived late for!

We can also develop a huge pull towards being unstructured if we constantly lived in difficult situations we had no control over. This is even more significant if it happened when we were still kids. If, as a child, we felt that we couldn't control our parent's tantrums or aggression, that we couldn't control our classmates from bullying us or that we couldn't stop our abuser, we learn that we have no control over our surroundings. As a result, we give up any attempt to control life. We just focus on living in the moment with no consideration of the future.

Another reason why we might strongly steer away from structure is if we were brought up in a very restrictive environment. Although overly controlling parents or a very rigid culture can result in becoming a very controlling person, the opposite can also be the case and we rebel against the pressure this exerts upon us. We move in the opposite direction and become completely carefree, unconsciously trying to stand our ground against that oppressive control we experienced.

Not trying to constantly control life has its benefits. But living only in a structureless manner also comes with its difficulties because we lose touch with some aspects of reality. We end up changing our desires, thoughts and decisions purely according to what we're feeling at that particular moment. As a result, we can easily feel panicked or overwhelmed. It also makes it harder to deal with everyday life demands. We forget to pay our bills on time or we overspend. We miss deadlines for assignments or we miss our train because we didn't check the travel time needed to get to the station. If we only respond in a reactive way to our emotions, it can also negatively impact our relationships. This makes it difficult to have the longer-term stability that some desire as we're constantly shifting from enmeshed love to explosive anger.

Living in a less structured manner can, at times, also lead us to adopt a more victim-like role in life. Because we feel that we have no control, we can sometimes believe that things are constantly happening to *us*. We end up interpreting what happens around us as intentionally directed at *us*. The train left on time, but we feel that it didn't wait for *us*. We were fined for parking in the wrong spot because the traffic warden was picking on *us*. This perspective leads us to believe that life is out to get us and that we're just at its mercy.

Being centred while letting go

Being fixated on control and being highly unstructured are two opposite poles of a spectrum with a lot of grey areas in between. Both sides are important for a healthy lifestyle. A less extreme version of being in control is to be centred. This is about being able to focus and to be grounded in the present moment. Unlike what happens when we live only in a structureless fashion, being centred allows us to stand on solid ground and face life with a deeper sense of inner strength. We're in touch with various aspects of reality, including the consequences of our actions and decisions. By being centred, we balance out our spontaneity without fixating ourselves on being in control.

On the other hand, a less extreme version of living in an unstructured way is to be able to let go. The difference between the two is that letting go entails a conscious choice, while living in a structureless manner implies allowing unconscious forces to steer our actions. By letting go, we take a flexible approach to life without acting out of our feelings of fear, anxiety or being overwhelmed.

The more we live out both being centred and letting go, the more able we are to live a well-balanced life. In this way, we remain open to what life brings to us while still being anchored enough in ourselves and the reality around us.

Learning how to be centred while letting go

The following are some ways that can help you become a more centred person.

- Be mindful of the present moment. Ground yourself in what's happening around you right now, in what you're thinking, feeling and sensing in your body.

- Focus on what you can actually control. List the things that you're really in control of when it comes to your health, appearance, emotional well-being, productivity and mental stimulation.

- Create a distance between yourself and what you feel you need to control. You can create this distance physically by moving away from something. You can also create it psychologically by imagining yourself physically distant from what you need to control and observing it from the outside rather than being immersed in it.

- Choose to deal with some difficulties that you're currently encountering at a future point in time rather than having to face everything now.

- Keep a dumping-journal. Use it to dump your unpleasant feelings on paper so as to decrease the need to control their outpouring when they accumulate.

- Make a conscious effort to try to accept uncertainty as part of life. We can never know the future because we're living in the present.

- Practise being self-compassionate.

The following are some ways to help you let go more.

- Learn to use your body to ground yourself in the present moment. Do a body scan as described in chapter 02 (p. 13). Do some yoga, Qi Gong, Tai Chi or a similar practice.

- Think before you act. Find some time to reflect on what you're feeling. Slow down your thinking process. Question and understand your emotions instead of just reacting to them. Ask yourself: What am I feeling? Why am I feeling this? What can I do with this feeling?

- Although you can have a gut feeling about something, it doesn't mean that all gut feelings are intuitions. Some are just based on biases or prejudices. Learn to distinguish between which gut feelings are intuition and which ones aren't.

- Control the stimuli you're surrounded by. Avoid being in situations where there's a lot going on and a lot of noise as these will distract you from what you're doing.

- Learn to manage your time. Make a general plan of your week on a Sunday and plan today for tomorrow.

- Group together small tasks that need doing and do them in one go.

- Regulate how much time you spend on social media. Set a time limit and stick to it. Otherwise, it's easy to get carried away.

- Find 10 minutes each day to organise your workspace and your home. The less clutter you have, the easier it is to be grounded in yourself and your surroundings instead of being distracted by every single thing you have lying around.

- Plan for the unexpected. Have some savings put aside, have spares of essential items and ensure that you can be physically safe (e.g. having a fire blanket in the kitchen).

- Clarify what your goals are. Break them down into achievable and measurable small tasks that you can keep track of.

- Establish a basic daily routine. It doesn't have to be set in stone, but it helps to structure your day.

The following exercises help you become more aware of how you approach control and structure in your life, explore how they developed in your life and offer you a space for becoming more balanced in your relationship with them.

How it relates to your life

How does this text relate to your life?
Write down anything that comes to mind, heart or body.

Exercises

01. The spectrum of control

✍ If you look at your life as a whole, where would you place yourself on the spectrum between being extremely controlling and being extremely unstructured? Mark this on the line below.

<——>

controlling   *unstructured*

02. The benefits of being who I am

✍ Look at your place on the spectrum in exercise 01. If you tend to be more in control, how does it help you? How does it make you a stronger person? If you tend to be more unstructured, how does it help you and make you stronger?

✍ Write down what you learnt about the benefits of being yourself when it comes to control and structure.

03. Looking at the other end of the spectrum

- Evaluate what your fears of being on the opposite end of the spectrum of control are. If you tend towards being unstructured, what are your fears about having more structure in your life? If you tend more towards control, what do you fear about letting go?
- Write down your fears in the space below.

❧❧   Now, think about the potential benefits of being on the opposite end of the spectrum to the one you're usually on.

❧❧   In the space below, write down the benefits that come to mind.

04. Imagining an alternative me

- Imagine yourself being more on the other side of the spectrum of control than where you usually are. Think about the following:
  - What kind of person would you be if you let go more or if you were more centred in your life?
  - How would you speak, what would you wear, how would you walk and behave?
  - What kind of work would you do?
  - What kind of friends would you have?
  - Where would you go out to have fun?
  - What hobbies would you have?
  - How would you have sex?
- List each different aspect you come up with in the table below in the column entitled 'Aspect'.

Aspect	Possible	Unsure	Impossible

- Now, look at each aspect and ask yourself what the likelihood of you becoming that kind of person is. In the boxes next to each aspect, mark whether you think it's possible for it to ever happen, whether you're unsure or whether you believe it's impossible.

05. Two things I can change

- Look at the items you marked as 'possible' in exercise 04. Choose the two most possible ones and write them down below in the column entitled 'Aspect', starting with the one you believe you can achieve more easily.

- Now, think of one way in which you can help yourself integrate each aspect into your everyday life. It might involve changing something you already do, engaging in a new sort of behaviour or modifying your thinking patterns.

Aspect	What I can do

06. A person I admire

- Is there a person that you admire who, in comparison to you, is more on the opposite side of the spectrum of control? What do you admire or like in their way of living life when it comes to being in control?

- List these qualities below.

____

𖤓 Pick one of their qualities that you would like to incorporate into your life and that's more important and achievable for you. Also decide on one action that you will take to change and incorporate this quality into your life.

Quality	What I can do

07. How I physically express control

- Notice how you use your body and how you're speaking during the day. People who want to be in control tend to have more rigid postures and make less use of the space around them. Those who are less structured tend to be the opposite. If you find it hard to remember to observe yourself during the day, set an hourly timer and check in with your body every time the alarm goes off. Just make sure you select a pleasant alarm sound!

- Write down what you've observed about how you use your body and how this reflects the importance of being in control or unstructured to you.

- When you look at how you use your body, is there anything that you would want to change about it? Maybe you want to loosen up a bit physically or to maintain a bit more composure.

- Pick one thing that you want to change and write it down in the space below. Try implementing it in your life.

08. The role of control throughout my life

The horizontal line below represents your life. Use the space above and below this line to sketch another line that represents how your tendency to be in control or unstructured has changed throughout your life. The further up you go on the graph, the more being in control has been important to you. The further down you go, the more being unstructured has been important to you.

- Look at the line you just sketched and take note of any substantial changes. Did anything significant happen at that time in your life?
- Write down what you noticed about how your relationship with control and structure has changed over time.

09. Comparing myself to my caregivers

- Think about your parents or significant adults who were around you while you were growing up. Where does each one of them lie on the spectrum between being controlling and being unstructured? Use a line for each one of them and mark with a cross how you experienced them at that time in your life.

Parent/significant adult:

controlling   *unstructured*

Parent/significant adult:

controlling   *unstructured*

Parent/significant adult:

controlling   *unstructured*

Parent/significant adult:

controlling   *unstructured*

❧ Look at the lines above and the one you marked for yourself in exercise 01. How do they compare? Can you think of any reasons why your line is similar or different to theirs?

----

10. **Moving freely with the music**

- If you tend to be in control, take off your shoes and start playing some music that's drum heavy, for example, Latin American or African drums. Allow your body to sway with the music. Start by allowing your arms to move haphazardly. Continue with your shoulders, torso, hips, legs, head and feet. Be random.

- Spend at least 10 to 15 minutes moving like this.

- In the end, stand still and notice your emotions and what you're sensing in your body.

- Take a note of what you observed about yourself.

11. Being a mountain

- If you tend to be more unstructured in life, find a place where you won't be disturbed.

- Stand in the mountain pose by standing with your legs hip-width apart, your back straight, your arms by your sides and with your face looking forwards.

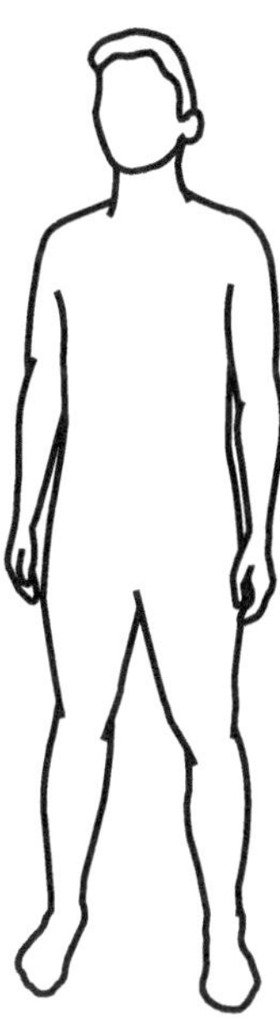

- Feel how your head pushes into your neck, into your shoulders, your spine, your hips, your legs and your feet.

- Notice what it feels like to sense this pressure moving down through your body.

- Now, imagine you're a mountain, steady and strong, and that nothing can move you: no snow, no rain, no sunshine, no wind.

- Notice how it feels to be in such a strong position. Does anything feel familiar or different to your current life? What can you draw from this experience and how can you integrate it into your life?

- Write about your experience of being a solid, strong being and what you can incorporate into your life to make it better.

____

____

____

____

____

____

____

____

____

____

____

____

____

____

____

____

12. To-do lists

∽ Think of the things you need to do.

∽ List them down in the table below according to whether they're urgent (they need to be done as soon as possible), important (they need to be done soon) or other.

∽ Examine each item in the 'Important' and 'Other' columns and, if you think an item can be done in less than 15 minutes, highlight or circle it.

❧ Complete the items in this order:
- First, complete the items in your 'Urgent' list.
- Next, do the highlighted items in the 'Important' list.
- Then, do the highlighted items in the 'Other' list.
- Next, complete the rest of the items in the 'Important' list.
- Finally, complete the rest of the items in the 'Other' list.

Urgent	Important	Other

Urgent	Important	Other

13. Urgency versus desire

- If you're a person who tends to be in control, make a list of ten things that you need to do.
- Mark which items are urgent (they absolutely need to be done as soon as possible) and do them.

Item	Urgent	Not urgent

<table>
<tr><td></td><td></td><td></td></tr>
<tr><td></td><td></td><td></td></tr>
<tr><td></td><td></td><td></td></tr>
<tr><td></td><td></td><td></td></tr>
<tr><td></td><td></td><td></td></tr>
<tr><td></td><td></td><td></td></tr>
</table>

- ❧ Now, instead of doing the other items on the list, put the list away.
- ❧ Find one thing that you would like to do today, something that's enjoyable and fun, that comes from desire rather than duty.
- ❧ Do it.
- ❧ Write down what you did and how you felt after doing it. How did it feel to put your list aside? What do you learn from this for your everyday life?

14. Wandering around

- ⚬ If you like to be in control, go out for a walk and get lost in a neighbourhood. Don't use your mobile or think about which corners to turn at. Just let your feet choose the direction and instead focus on observing what's around you in detail.

- ⚬ When you finish your walk, take some time to reflect on your emotions and thoughts during and after the walk.

- ⚬ Write down what you learnt about the experience of being present with your surroundings instead of focusing on decision-making.

15. Timeless

- If you tend to be more in control, after you finish your work or study commitments for the day, check if you need to set the alarm for the next morning. If so, set the alarm and then put away your clock or watch or put your mobile phone on silent.

- Do whatever you want or need to do during the rest of the day according to how you feel. Don't plan when to do it. Eat when you feel hungry, walk your dog for as long as you feel like and sleep when you feel tired.

- Write about your experience of living an evening without having the clock regulate your behaviour. What did you learn about how you use time and planning? What did you notice about your awareness of your bodily needs? Can you do anything differently in your everyday life to take this more on board?

16. Week plan

- If you tend to be more unstructured, try to formulate a general plan for your week.

- This Sunday, find 20 minutes to plan the coming week.

- Use the plan below or create a different one that suits you better. It helps to divide each day into four sections (morning, afternoon, evening, night) to allow for flexibility while still maintaining some basic structure.

- Use a pencil to write down one activity you'll do in each box.

- If the time comes and you need to do something else, erase it and write that activity down in another part of the week.

- Ensure that you stick to doing at least one of the planned activities each day.

Date	Morning	Afternoon	Evening	Night
Monday				
Tuesday				
Wednesday				

Thursday				
Friday				
Saturday				
Sunday				

17. Stop and listen

- If you prefer living with less structure, ensure that, when you meet the next person, you only talk after the other person has stopped talking for at least 3 seconds.

- During those 3 seconds, notice any body sensations you have or any emotions you're feeling.

- Afterwards, reflect on the conversation you had with that person. Note down your emotions and body sensations. Write about what it felt like to wait before speaking. Did it change anything in how the conversation developed and in how you communicated with the other person?

13

ON BEING GOOD AND NOT-SO-GOOD

Most of us are familiar with the yin-yang symbol: the half-black-half-white circle. It symbolises that everything exists in conjunction with its opposite and that opposites complement each other – light only exists with darkness, the old with the young. Life is about finding a balance somewhere in between, a balance that includes both opposites to different degrees.

In Western cultures, we look at opposites in a very black-and-white way. It's either one side or the other. We favour young age and young bodies. We favour the rich and the able-bodied, the gender-conforming and socially compliant. Because of our black-and-white thinking, we end up judging the two opposites. Our preferences become the 'good' ones, in contrast to their 'bad' counterparts.

Audio files for this chapter can be accessed at
thehorsesmouth.michaelconti.net/lbwy-ch13
or by scanning the adjacent QR code.

For a number of us, being good becomes, in itself, something to aspire to. Given that the best confirmation that we're a 'good person' comes from the way other people react to us, we often try to please others. We become the 'good child' when we're young, the 'good employee' at our workplace. And, should we become parents, we imagine that we can be all-loving towards our children. In this way, our parents, our boss or our children will validate us as being a 'good person'. This dynamic can push some of us not only to be good but perfect, as being good is not even good enough.

However, light only exists with shadow. And so, our 'good' side always co-exists with our 'not-so-good' one.

The 'bad child'

The 'not-so-good' side to ourselves is present in all of us even if we don't like acknowledging it. In some of us, it can end up taking the upper hand. We become the rebel child, the difficult employee, the self-centred or highly critical parent. It can lead us to take a hostile stance towards any form of authority. We become self-absorbed, focused only on our desires and not caring about the ones around us. We become embittered and resentful people, full of jealousy and hatred.

Maybe, when we were kids, the adults around us explicitly encouraged us to act out from our 'not-so-good' side. Or we were mainly surrounded by adults who were usually angry and unloving and so we learnt that this is how people usually behave. Maybe being a 'bad child' was the only way to get the attention we desperately craved. After all, adults often pay more attention to misbehaviour than to any good-doing! Or we learnt to be the 'bad child' in order to protect ourselves from violence or helplessness, as happens when one becomes the bully after having been bullied themselves or experienced a deep lack of being loved.

The 'good child'

For those of us who were more of a 'good child', this was probably due to the fact that we learnt to please the adults around us in order to get their love and protection. Being lively, noisy or mischievous resulted in reprimands. Misbehaviour led to adults telling us that, if we behave in such a way, they won't love us, with all the guilt and anxiety that this generates. If, on the other hand, we were obedient and we satisfied the adults' expectations, we were showered with love and affection and told that we were a 'good boy' or a 'good girl'. We learnt that, in order to be loved, we need to please others.

However, what we also probably learnt in the process was to repress the negative emotions and impulses that others don't like in us. We 'forgot' that they're part of us. As a result, we end up unconsciously trying to convince ourselves that our 'not-so-good' side doesn't exist. We become blind to its presence. But this doesn't actually get rid of it. Instead, it ends up acting independently, outside of our awareness. For example, we might be annoyed by some things that our partner does at home, but we struggle to acknowledge this annoyance as it clashes with our feeling of love for them. Because the annoyance remains hidden, it can fester and lead to a subtle sense of bitterness that can make us more critical towards them. Another example is when sexual desires or attractions are repressed during one's development because they go against what is deemed acceptable or desirable. Often, they end up blowing up later in life, resulting in a huge identity crisis and strongly impacting one's relationships and well-being.

The challenge

Some of us end up getting so entangled in being the 'good child' or the 'bad child' that it becomes our identity in adulthood. It ends up defining us and so we cannot risk including its opposite because, if we do so, we jeopardise our identity. If we change who we are, we fear losing the way we perceive ourselves and interact with others. We lose the security of what we know. If, as a 'bad person', we start including the 'good' side into our identity, we fear that we'll be ignored or taken advantage of. And if, as a 'good person', we start incorporating the 'not-so-good' side into our identity, we fear being judged as unlovable and being rejected. Consequently, it can be very challenging to incorporate the opposite dimension into our life.

Striking a balance

Regardless of whether we like it or not, both the 'good' and the 'not-so-good' sides are part of us. Usually, they're not morally good or bad in themselves. They're characteristics, impulses and desires to which we attribute a moral quality. By doing so, it gives us even more reason to live out one side rather than the other. For example, if we judge the feelings of anger or lust as 'bad', we will try to block them off. However, these are just emotions and desires that we cannot help feeling and they aren't good or bad in themselves. On the other hand, if we label submitting to authority as 'good', we will tend to obey blindly. Consequently, we risk losing our personal power and our ability to be critical of what's demanded of us. We become blind followers in the herd. This can result in many problematic situations ranging from accepting anything that our partner demands from us to even harming others in a cold and heartless manner because we're just obeying orders.

Instead of choosing to live only as a 'good person' or a 'bad person' and thereby amputating the other side of ourselves, we need to learn to recognise both sides, incorporate them into our identity and use them whenever necessary. Otherwise, we risk living an unbalanced life, oblivious to what's happening outside of our awareness.

Being a 'good person' is crucial for us to function in society because, as social animals, we need to relate to one another. There's a degree of adjustment to other people that's essential when establishing good social relations. Being in a group isn't just about me. So, adopting a negative approach will only result in me being alienated from the group. At the same time, it's also important to connect to our 'not-so-good' side. This allows us to safeguard our needs and keeps us from being hurt. It stops others from trampling over us. It protects us from emotional pain. Incorporating the 'not-so-good' side of ourselves isn't the same as intentionally harming others. Instead, it's about acknowledging and accepting every aspect of ourselves. How we decide to act following that is another matter.

How to incorporate the 'good' and the 'not-so-good'

The following are some suggestions that can help you be more balanced in life by incorporating both the 'good' and the 'not-so-good' sides of yourself.

- Check whether you're aware of emotions you feel that are often judged negatively, such as anger, jealousy or hatred. Check whether you believe that it's wrong to feel irritation or hatred towards people who love you or whom you love. Remember that you cannot control your emotions. You can only control the actions you take.

- When you witness bad behaviour in others, check whether you acknowledge the same tendencies in yourself.

- Try noticing in which situations you become the 'good person' and in which ones you become the 'bad person'. Do you notice that you try to be the 'good person' to compensate for an aspect of yourself or a desire you have that you judge as being 'bad'? Or vice versa?

- Consider what the benefits might be of being the opposite of who you tend to be. And think about how you can profit by incorporating some of your opposite into your life.

The exercises that follow aim at helping you develop more awareness around the 'good' and 'not-so-good' sides of yourself and how these have developed throughout your life. They also provide you with an opportunity to further integrate both into your everyday life.

How it relates to your life

How does this text relate to your life?
Write down anything that comes to mind, heart or body.

Exercises

01. Drawing my 'good' and 'bad' selves

ઉ໐   Imagine what your 'good' self looks like. Draw it in the space below.

My 'Good' Self

ᔆ Do the same with your 'bad' self.

My 'Bad' Self

My 'Bad' Self

❧ Look at your drawings. Notice the shapes, colours and sizes that you used. Write down your interpretation of what this shows you about those aspects of yourself and how you relate to them.

02. Who am I and when?

❧ Think about which side of yourself is usually present in the following situations. Is it your 'good' side or your 'not-so-good' side?

❧ Next to each situation, there's a line that indicates the spectrum between being 'good' and 'not-so-good'. For each situation, check with yourself which side you tend to show more of. Mark this on the line with a cross.

Being with your family

'good' ⟵————————————————⟶ *'not-so-good'*

Being with close friends

'good' ⟵————————————————⟶ *'not-so-good'*

Meeting acquaintances

'good' ⟵————————————————⟶ *'not-so-good'*

At the workplace

'good' ⟵————————————————⟶ *'not-so-good'*

Relationships with other people

'good' ⟵————————————————⟶ *'not-so-good'*

How you see yourself

'good' ⟵————————————————⟶ *'not-so-good'*

Your sex life

'good' ⟵————————————————⟶ *'not-so-good'*

Your creative side

'good' ⟵————————————————⟶ *'not-so-good'*

Arguing with someone
you care about

'good' ⟵————————————————⟶ *'not-so-good'*

Disagreeing with others

'good' ⟵————————————————⟶ *'not-so-good'*

Feeling angry

'good' ⟵————————————————⟶ *'not-so-good'*

Feeling anxious

'good' ⟵————————————————⟶ *'not-so-good'*

Feeling sad

'good' ⟵————————————————⟶ *'not-so-good'*

Feeling afraid

'good' ⟵————————————————⟶ *'not-so-good'*

Feeling tired

'good' ⟵————————————————⟶ *'not-so-good'*

03. Two highly irritating people

∽ Bring to mind two people you know whom you find highly irritating.

∽ Write down their qualities or behaviours that irritate you.

Person	Irritating qualities and behaviours

∽ Take some time to reflect on how those qualities are, in some way, also present in you. They're probably qualities or behaviours that you keep hidden or wish that you could have or do. Write down what comes up for you in the space below. What does this teach you about how you project undesirable sides of yourself onto others?

____

____

____

____

____

____

____

____

04. Matching opposites

- In the table below, write a list of your positive qualities.
- In the column next to them, list their opposites.
- Identify how you live out the opposite of your positive qualities in your everyday life and write this down in the last column.

Positive quality	Opposite quality	How I live out the opposite quality

෴ Write down your observations about how you live out the hidden and opposite side of your positive qualities.

05. The hidden aspects

෴ If you tend to be more of a 'good person', think about any of your 'not-so-good' desires that you judge negatively or that you keep hidden from others.

෴ If you tend to be more of a 'bad person', think about any of your 'good' qualities that you try to avoid having others see in you.

෴ In the space below, write down your observations about this.

06. Facing my opposite side

- Place two chairs in front of each other and sit in one of them.

- Imagine that the opposite side of yourself is sitting on the chair in front of you. If you're more of a 'good person', imagine that sitting in front of you is your 'not-so-good' side, and vice versa. Notice what that side looks like and how it's sitting.

- Get in touch with what it feels like to be sitting in front of your opposite. What thoughts do you have about it? How does it physically feel to be sitting there, so close, directly in front of it?

- Once you've connected to your physical sensation and your emotions, see whether you would like to change the position of the chairs. Once you do so, sit down again and notice what you think and how you feel in relation to the other chair. Notice any difference in how you physically feel in relation to that side of yourself now that it's in a different place.

- Repeat this exercise as often as necessary until you no longer notice any particular shift in your emotions and physical sensations.

- Write down what you learnt from this exercise about facing the opposite side of yourself.

07. Pros and cons

- Think about ways in which you act as a 'good person' or a 'bad person'. List these in the first column of the table below.

- Think about how each action benefits you. Write this down in the second column entitled 'How it helps me'.

- Finally, think about three ways in which each behaviour hinders you from developing further. Write this down in the last column.

How I act	How it helps me	How it hinders me

08. What stops me

- Spend some time thinking about the fears or guilt feelings that stop you from further incorporating your opposite side. List them in the space below.

- After you look at your list, write down what you learnt about the biggest obstacles that stop you from changing.

09. Floating back into my past

- Go over the memories of your childhood and adolescence. What are your strongest and earliest memories of being the 'good child' or the 'bad child'? How do you feel now about who you were back then?

- Use the space below to note down your memories and what they bring up for you nowadays.

10. **Who liked and disliked me**

- Look at the memories in exercise 09 and recall the people who were around you at that time of your life, especially the adults.

- Think about who liked you as you were and who didn't. In what way did they show that they liked or disliked you as being 'good' or 'not-so-good'?

- Think about how you benefited from being who you were with them. Why was it better to be 'good' or 'not-so-good'? What might have happened had you been the opposite of that?

- Finally, think about how those people benefited from you being the 'good child' or the 'bad child'.

- Use the space below to note down what you learnt about how the people you were surrounded by impacted how you developed the 'good' and 'not-so-good' sides of yourself.

11. A large reminder

- If you tend more towards being on the 'good' side, find a large sheet of paper and write down in large letters: "I don't have to be perfect!" or something similar that's more meaningful for you.

- If you tend more towards being on the 'not-so-good' side, do the same with the phrase: "I am also a good person!" or something similar.

- Hang it up somewhere in your house or workplace where it's easy to see. Look at it as frequently as possible and repeat it to yourself.

12. Switching between extremes

- Stand in front of a mirror.

- Focus on the kind of person you usually are, on whether you live more from the 'good' or the 'not-so-good' side of yourself. Notice any emotions or physical sensations you get when you focus on this.

- While looking at yourself in the mirror, start changing your facial expression using gestures or movement to show this 'good' or 'not-so-good' side of yourself. Amplify your expressions or gestures to the maximum. For example, if you tend to please others, you might start by smiling and then amplify this to a very wide grin. If you tend to live mostly as a frustrated person, you might start by frowning and then end up grinding your teeth and clenching your fists.

- Notice how you feel when your body amplifies your typical 'good' or 'not-so-good' side and any physical sensations that accompany it.

- Now, start shifting your expression and your gestures to the opposite of being 'good' or 'not-so-good' while still looking at yourself. For example, if you had a wide grin on your face, start changing it to a very big frown while clenching your fists.

- Notice what it feels like to physically become the opposite of who you typically are. Stay with this feeling for a while. Notice any physical sensations and any thoughts that come up for you.

- Continue switching between your opposing sides while noticing your feelings and body sensations.

Write about your experience of being an extreme version of yourself and its opposite. What does this teach you about yourself?

13. Dear hidden side ...

- Bring to mind the 'good' or 'not-so-good' side of yourself that you feel has been mostly absent in your life.

- Use the space below or another sheet of paper to write a letter to this side of yourself. This is an open letter so there's no fixed format. You might want to express how you feel about that side of yourself and why it's easier for you to avoid it. Reflect upon what you think it needs and what it fears, as well as what you're afraid might happen if it were to become a more integral part of your life. You might also want to express your desires in relation to that hidden side of yourself. Write down anything else that you need or want in relation to this.

- After you write your letter, check in with your emotions and physical sensations. You might want to do something symbolic with the letter, like burning it, keeping it on display in your room or putting it in a sealed envelope. Base your decision on what you feel would bring this letter-writing moment to a good closure.

14. Stealing from someone else

- Bring to mind someone you know who manages to live their 'good' and 'not-so-good' sides in a more balanced and integrated way than you do. Pick one thing that they do differently from you and write it down in the space below.

- Try doing it yourself in the coming week.

- Use the following table to monitor how you feel after each time you act in this new way. Pay attention to your emotions, thoughts and physical sensations.

Day	What I did	How I felt afterwards	My reflections

Day	What I did	How I felt	My reflections

- ✍ Feel free to repeat this exercise for a longer period of time or to try out another kind of behaviour.

- ✍ Look back at how you've behaved differently and what your feelings were. Write down what you've learnt about the process of changing yourself by trying a new behaviour.

____

____

____

____

____

15. One single action

- If you tend more towards being on the 'good' side, pick something a bit more on the 'not-so-good' side of life and choose to do it once. It can be a very simple thing, such as not brushing your hair before you go out or crossing the street when the lights are red (and there aren't cars around).

- If you tend more towards being on the 'not-so-good' side, choose a good action to perform and do it once. Pick up a piece of rubbish from the pavement and throw it in the bin or wash the plates for someone else if you don't usually do that.

After taking this action, check in with yourself and notice how you feel afterwards. What does this show you about the possibility of incorporating the other side of yourself? Write down your observations in the space below.

16. A three-way conversation with the 'good' and the 'bad'

- Set up three chairs in a circle.

- Sit on one of the chairs. This chair represents you as a whole person.

- Imagine your 'good' side sitting on one of the other chairs and your 'not-so-good' side sitting on the third chair.

- Notice what you feel when you're sitting in front of both of them.

- Now, think of what you want to tell your 'good' side. You might want to talk to it about how you feel about it, any memories you have, any regrets or desires. You might have questions you want to ask in order to understand it more, questions about what it needs, wants or fears. Imagine that you're speaking directly to it. Don't just think about what you want to say – speak aloud.

- Next, go and sit down on the chair representing the 'good' side.

- Notice how it feels to hear what was just said. How would you like to respond as the 'good' side? Speak directly to the chair that you were sitting on, the one that represents you as a whole person.

- Go back to that first chair. Observe how it feels to hear the reply you just got. Is there anything else you want to say back? Again, speak aloud, directly addressing the chair.

- Next, focus on the other chair, the one representing your 'not-so-good' side, and repeat the exercise. What would you like to say to this side of yourself? Again, say this aloud.

- Go and sit down on the chair representing the 'not-so-good' side of yourself and notice how it feels to be sitting on that chair and hearing what was just said. Formulate your reply and say it aloud.

- Go back to the first chair and again notice how it feels to hear that reply from the 'not-so-good' side. See what you want to say back to it and say it aloud.

- See if there's anything else that either of these two sides of yourself wants to say. Maybe the 'good' side wants to say something to the 'not-so-good' side, or vice versa. Or you want to have a longer conversation with one of them. The important thing is to always sit in the chair that represents that side of yourself. End the exercise sitting on the chair that represents you as a whole person.

- ᔕ Finally, take some time to reflect on what came up for you during the exercise. Notice any emotions, thoughts or physical sensations.
- ᔕ In the space below, write about your experience. What came up for you? What did you learn about yourself and your different sides? How can you use self-talk as a way of interacting with these different sides of yourself?

14

ON SAFETY AND VULNERABILITY

Can you remember a situation where you felt unsafe or insecure? Or when you felt exposed and vulnerable? Maybe it was because of how someone spoke to you or how they acted towards you. Maybe there was something physically threatening. Can you recall what helped you reduce your stress level and feel safe again? Regardless of what form they actually take, we experience vulnerability and lack of safety as threats to our survival. And as described in chapter 05, any perceived threat triggers the amygdala, which in turn activates our stress response.

Different forms of threat

The threats that we experience can be of three different forms. The first is when something happens in our body, like when we feel a sudden pain in our belly. The second is when something happens to us from the

Audio files for this chapter can be accessed at **thehorsesmouth.michaelconti.net/lbwy-ch14** *or by scanning the adjacent QR code.*

outside, like when we're almost run over by a car or we're fired from our job. The third is when we feel isolated because, as mammals, we perceive this as a threat to our survival as much as the other two forms of threat.

Decreasing the sense of threat

Being in a constant state of threat is not sustainable for us so, when the threat is over, we seek means to calm ourselves down again. We tend to do this in three different ways.

The fight-or-flight response

As described in chapter 05, one way in which we try to decrease the sense of threat is by activating the fight-or-flight response. We either move away from the threat or we directly try to get rid of it. If it's a temporary threat, the moment it's no longer there makes it possible for the threat centre in our brain to relax. This signals to the body that it can do the same. However, some threats can last for a long time, like if we experience neglect or poor care as children or if we're in a very stressful long-term relationship. In these cases, our in-built stress response system struggles to handle stress in the normal way. We end up feeling unsafe for too long a period of time and so our stress response gets overloaded and never switches off. This leaves us in a chronic state of stress.

Finding a safer space

A second way in which we try to decrease the sense of threat is to engage with something that offers us the opposite of stress – a sense of safety. We find a shoulder to cry on, someone to give us a hug or we do some yoga or breathing exercises that help our body relax. In these situations, we create a space where we feel safe. By doing so, we feel calmer and so decrease the activity in the threat centre of our brain. Consequently, our mind stops fearing that our survival is at risk.

Nevertheless, our way of judging the safety of a situation isn't fool-proof. We don't compare different situations objectively but according to how we feel about them. We might have learnt to value some forms of safety as more important than others and this can lead us to ignore the price we pay in the process. We end up accepting unhealthy behaviours or relationships because we judge them as better than something else that we perceive as more threatening. For example, we might be too afraid of leaving an abusive relationship because the prospect of being alone feels scarier than being with someone who treats us in an abusive manner.

Worrying and obsessing

A third way in which we try to decrease the sense of threat is to behave or think in ways that give us a feeling of control – albeit a false one – over reality. By feeling in control over one aspect of life, we decrease the stress we feel around not being in control over other aspects. For example, we might develop a strong need to always have things in order or to make sure that everything is spotlessly clean. Or we might feel that we need to ensure that we complete every single task that we started. We might hoard things that we definitely don't need or habitually worry about something bad happening to us or to people we love even though the objective chance of that happening is extremely low.

We might even recognise these behaviours or thoughts as irrational. And yet, we feel enslaved by them. The reason why these behaviours and thought patterns have such a strong grip on us is that we've learnt that they make us feel safe. Initially, they used to diminish or switch off our stress response. But now that we're adults, these behaviours and thought patterns no longer help us. On the contrary, they make other aspects of our lives more difficult!

It's important to understand these dynamics so that we don't end up having unrealistic expectations of ourselves or be highly self-critical when we act in these ways. Instead, by better understanding our behaviour, we can adopt a gentler approach with ourselves. After all, what our brain is trying to do is to avoid threat in the way it knows best. Making ourselves feel worse will only end up strengthening the sense of threat!

Vulnerability

One thing that easily triggers the sense of threat is when we feel vulnerable. Vulnerability can be experienced in various situations. It can be of a more psychological nature, like when we're about to attend a party and perhaps feeling anxious about being around new people. It can also be experienced in our body, especially when it no longer functions in the way it used to, like if we're severely ill, we've been involved in a serious accident or we're growing older.

By being vulnerable, we open ourselves up to the possibility of being hurt. To ensure our safety, our mind errs on the side of caution, often turning the possibility that we *can* be hurt into a probability that we *will* be. It also steers us away from the possibility of being vulnerable. However, by doing so, our behaviours end up being primarily determined by the possibility of danger.

Trying hard to avoid vulnerability comes with its own set of problems. First of all, being vulnerable is intrinsic to being alive. Our mind is very much aware that, as long as we're alive, there's the possibility of death. However, incessantly thinking about death would overwhelm the threat centre in our brain and so we often disregard that aspect of reality. The problem here lies with the fact that, by ignoring the eventuality of death, we can end up being robbed of the possibility of making the right decisions, the ones that make our lives matter. Being in touch with our vulnerability allows us to know our real strength and live a life where we're more connected to ourselves, others and our surroundings. It stops us from being in a state of constant avoidance and alienation. It gives us the chance to deal better with stress by actively deciding what we want to do and being unapologetically ourselves. By choosing to be vulnerable, we prevent the threat centre of our brain from deciding things for us every time we encounter something different to the usual.

The second problem with avoiding vulnerability concerns our relationships. The more we act out of the fear of being vulnerable, the stronger the need to avoid real connection with others or to manipulate our relationships in order to feel secure. Although this can provide an initial sense of safety, it actually undermines our relationships. We end up increasing the chances of others abandoning us or we end up never having truly lived out our relationships. Both of these can make us feel fundamentally unhappy. Instead of behaving in this way, we would be better off developing further our inner sense of security so that it doesn't depend entirely on our relationships. Such an inner sense of security enables us to be stronger in our vulnerability, thus being able to face life with all its challenges.

Being internally secure while still being vulnerable

The following are some ways that can help you develop an inner sense of security without running away from vulnerability.

- Increase your awareness of how your childhood experiences have formed the way you relate to others. Observe how you repeat these patterns in your current life so you can identify what you need to change.

- Look out for your safety behaviours, those that make you feel secure even though they're not linked to the actual threat, like staying in your room all day because the day before your partner was a bit irritated with you.

- Acknowledge that you're not superhuman and that you have your flaws and dark sides. Accept that you can never get rid of these.

- Don't run away from moments where you feel vulnerable. Stay with the feeling of vulnerability. You'll notice that you can survive it and, thus, emerge stronger.

- Stop trying to prove that you're worthwhile. Otherwise, people won't be interested in who you are but in what you offer.

- Stop putting yourself down and dismissing compliments.

- Share with others what you feel insecure and vulnerable about. It will make you feel stronger – a paradox that works!

- Let people know clearly and unapologetically what you think and desire. Being respectful and being yourself aren't mutually exclusive. On the contrary, they're very close allies!

- Align your behaviour with your values.

The following exercises are aimed at helping you understand your sense of security and how you live out vulnerability while finding ways of further developing both aspects of your life.

How it relates to your life

How does this text relate to your life?
Write down anything that comes to mind, heart or body.

Exercises

01. Foetal position

- ❧ Curl up into a foetal position, making sure that you're as comfortable as possible.

- ❧ Stay in this position for a few minutes. With every inhale, notice what it feels like to be in that position.

- ❧ Notice where in your body you feel a sense of safety and security. Notice what the sensation feels like. Is it warm or cool, large or small, throbbing or tingling? Does it feel like it's moving upwards or downwards, or is it immobile? Are there any other things you notice about it?

- ❧ With the next few breaths, adjust your position to strengthen your feeling of safety.

- ❧ Take a number of deeper breaths and let them sink into your body, into that place of safety that you're feeling.

- ❧ Write down where the sense of safety is located in your body and what it feels like. What did you learn from this exercise about your experience of safety?

---

02. Safety behaviours and thought patterns

- Take some time to reflect on your safety behaviours and thought patterns, those you engage in so as to feel more secure. Don't judge yourself in relation to them. Remember that their aim is, ultimately, to make you feel safe.

- For each safety behaviour or thought pattern, ask yourself: What is my biggest fear of what might happen if I don't behave or think in that way?

Safety behaviour or thought pattern	My biggest fear if I don't engage in it

⁋ Continue your reflection over a few days, taking some time at the end of each day to notice your behaviours and thought patterns. Notice how frequently you tend to engage in them by noting it down in the table below.

Safety behaviour or thought pattern	Day of the week	Frequency

✎ Write down what you learnt about the link between your fears and your safety behaviours or thought patterns and how you engage in them.

____

____

____

____

____

____

____

03. Vulnerability and safety in my relationships

ℴ Think about your current, latest or most significant relationship you've had. You can think of a relationship with a very important friend instead of a romantic relationship. Reflect on the following questions and write your observations in the space below.

- In what ways do/did you try to feel safer in your relationship?
- In what ways do/did you clearly or subtly avoid being vulnerable?
- In what ways do/did you allow yourself to be more vulnerable in your relationship?

⇛ What do you feel when you look back at what you wrote? Is there anything that you would want to change?

⇛ Choose whether you want to take an extra step forwards and share some or all of the things that came up for you while doing this exercise with your partner or a very close friend.

⇛ Write down your reflections about how you experienced safety and vulnerability in relationships and the experience of sharing this with someone else.

04. My secure past

- Find a time when you can be quiet and undisturbed. Bring to mind any moment in your life when you felt the most secure. Was there any particular person or location with whom or where you felt that sense of security the most?

- Close your eyes and visualise the person or location.

- While talking aloud, describe them in the greatest level of detail that you possibly can.

- Notice how it feels to be focusing on them. You might feel that you're back in that moment in time, in that place or with that person. What feelings are you noticing now as you picture them? Do you detect any pleasant sensation in your body and, if so, where do you notice it? What does it feel like? Is the sensation solid or soft, warm or cool, rough or smooth? Does it have any shape or colour?

- Write about your memory of the person or location that made you feel safe and the emotions and body sensations that you experienced as you visualised them. How can you use this exercise to increase your inner sense of security?

____

____

____

____

____

____

____

____

____

____

____

____

____

____

05. Recollections of past difficult experiences

- Find some quiet time in a place where you won't be disturbed. Plan to do something pleasant after this exercise, like sipping a drink you particularly enjoy, doing some physical exercise or reading a book you really like.

- Reflect on the following questions:
    - Can you recall your earliest memories of when you felt unsafe, insecure or very vulnerable?
    - How did you live out those experiences? Did you express the feeling of insecurity and vulnerability to somebody else or did you hold it all inside of you?

- Were others present when you felt like that? How did they react? Did they understand you and empathise with you, or did they shame or punish you?

- At the end of the exercise, spend a few minutes thanking yourself for being strong and having come out the other end of such a situation. Follow this with the pleasant activity you planned initially.

- Write down what you learnt about your past experiences in relation to feeling secure and the people who were around you.

06. Feelings and sensations about my past

- Find some quiet time in a place where you won't be disturbed and plan on doing something pleasant after the exercise.

- **WARNING:** If during this exercise you notice that you start getting a very strong negative reaction, stop the exercise and use calming techniques as described in chapter 02 (p. 9). Then, engage in the pleasant thing you planned on doing.

- Start the exercise by bringing to mind any upsetting or traumatic experience you encountered when you were younger. It could have been something that happened to you or to someone else. It could have been something that actually happened or that there was a possibility of it happening. Examples of such experiences include growing up in physically dangerous environments, meeting abusive, manipulative or neglectful significant adults, being bullied or having an aspect of your identity that's negatively judged or discriminated against by others.

- Reflect on the following questions:
  - How does it feel to recall such experiences?
  - What do you notice in your body as you bring them to mind? Do you notice any stronger unpleasant sensations, like tension or pressure? Do you notice any disconnection from your body or any feeling of numbness?
  - How do you think these experiences affected your sense of safety and your ability to be vulnerable?
  - Is there anything you normally do to help you feel better when you recall such experiences? How helpful are these activities you engage in? Is there a downside to them? If so, is there any alternative that could be more beneficial and still allow you to not be consumed by a sense of insecurity?

- At the end of the exercise, close your eyes. Imagine the experience turning into a black-and-white image, getting smaller and distancing itself from you. Meanwhile, start focusing more on your breathing. Notice what kind of surface you're lying on, how your body is exerting pressure onto it and how that surface is pushing you back. Notice this in detail, paying attention to every part of your body.

- Congratulate yourself for being a strong person and still being alive.

- End the exercise by engaging in the pleasant thing you planned on doing.
- Write down your reflections on your emotional and bodily reactions to such difficult memories and your ways of surviving the upsetting feelings that they generate in you.

07. Hugging myself

- Sit, lie down or stand comfortably. Adopt a position where you're hugging yourself as shown in the following image.

- Notice if you feel any sense of care, protection or security in your body. Notice where it's located and its intensity. Take a few deep breaths and let them reach that sensation in your body, kindling it, nourishing it, strengthening it.

- Now, imagine that with every additional breath you take the sensation of security starts expanding slowly. Continue breathing into it while it expands until it fills all of your body.

- If there are moments in life when you feel overwhelmed, go back to this posture and allow yourself to reconnect with the physical sensation of safety.

- Write down what you learnt from this exercise about how you experience the sense of security in your body, taking note of how you can use it in moments when you feel overwhelmed.

---

08. The magical shape

- Close your eyes and visualise a magical shape, such as a sphere, that's invisible to everybody else. This shape protects whoever is inside it from anything that lies outside.

- Notice its colour, its texture, how transparent it is, the thickness of its wall. What does it feel like when you touch it? What is the temperature of its surface? What happens to it when you push it? What about when it bumps into other things?

- Now, step into the shape knowing that, once you're inside it, you're safe from everything and everybody else.

- Notice what it looks like from the inside. Is it the same as what it looks like from the outside? Does its surface feel the same on the inside? What about the temperature and lighting inside?

- Connect to the emotions that come up as you are inside this magical shape that will not allow anybody or anything else in unless you want it to.

- While keeping the image of the magical shape in your mind, draw your attention to your breathing. Notice the deepest point in your body that your breath reaches. Connect to that part of your body.

- Now, imagine that the wall of your magical shape is connected to that part of your body. With every breath you take in, feel the air reaching that part of your body and connecting to the wall of your shape making it stronger.

- Continue noticing the deeper sense of safety that you feel as you breathe in, connecting to your shape and feeling it grow stronger.

- While still picturing yourself inside your magical shape, imagine that far away from you lies something or someone that generates unpleasant emotions in you. Look at it as it moves towards you, as it reaches the outside of the magical shape and tries to penetrate it but doesn't succeed. Notice how the magical shape reacts to it, how it acts to protect you.

- Connect to your breathing, sensing the breath as it reaches that deepest part of your body and connects to the wall of the magical shape making it stronger, keeping out the unpleasant person, thing or event.

- Finally, picture that unpleasant person, thing or event retreating into the horizon. Stay inside your magical shape for a little longer. How does it feel to be protected by this magical shape while facing what you find unpleasant? In the end, step out of your shape.

- Use this exercise in moments when you feel that something is affecting you negatively or is triggering your sense of danger or threat. Visualise the magical shape surrounding you with its wall standing between you and what's negatively affecting you. Focus on your breathing, imagining it strengthening the wall of your magical shape.

⅋ Write down a detailed description of your shape, how your breath and your body sensations are connected to the wall of your shape and how it feels to be protected inside it.

09. Keeping bad experiences in the past

- Look back at the difficult experiences that came to mind previously in exercises 05 and 06. You might also have other experiences in mind.

- Close your eyes and picture one of those experiences.

- Now, imagine the image getting smaller as it moves back, away from you. Watch it until it becomes very tiny or disappears. If that danger is no longer around you nowadays, remind yourself that what happened in that experience lies in your past and that you're now safe.

- Formulate a statement of safety. For example, you might say: "That experience belongs in my past. I am now safe." Say this out loud to yourself. Repeat this, each time increasing the strength and volume of your voice.

- What do you notice about what you're thinking, how you're feeling and how you're holding your body throughout this exercise? How does the statement of safety affect you?

- Write down what you noticed about the possibility of putting the past in the past and how you can use the statement of safety in your everyday life.

10. Vulnerable in nature

- Go to a place in nature where there's a large open space, like on top of a hill or on the beach. Preferably, choose a day when it's quite windy and perhaps also raining. If you cannot go to an open space, try imagining being in that situation.

- Stand still for some minutes. Feel the wind blowing, the rain pelting you. Take note of how small you are in the world when facing the force of nature.

- Stay in that place for a while, feeling your vulnerability in the face of nature. Whenever you feel fear creeping up, take a couple of deep, slow breaths and remind yourself that you can withstand this because you're a strong person.

- Write about your experience and what you learnt about your ability to stay with your vulnerability.

11. Stepping into the insecure

- Use the following table to make a list of things you feel less safe or secure doing.

- Rate each item according to how secure or safe you feel about doing it. Use a scale of 0 (least safe/secure) to 10 (safest/most secure).

What I feel insecure or less safe doing	How safe/secure I feel about doing it (0-10)

❧ Now, choose the item with the highest score – one you feel quite safe or secure in doing – and commit to doing it. Write it down below.

I commit myself to do the following:

✍ Decide on which day and at what time you will do this. Before and after you do it, check with how you're feeling and write down your emotions in the table below.

✍ Repeat this a few more times, keeping note of any changes you observe in your emotions.

Day	What I felt before	What I felt afterwards

- ✺ Look back at the initial list. Is there something else that you want to try out, maybe one with a lower score?

- ✺ Write about the changes you noticed in yourself when doing something you feel a bit more insecure or unsafe about. What does this teach you about how you can act to face your insecurity?

12. Opening up on my own

- ઐ Curl up into a foetal position as illustrated in exercise 01, making sure that you're as comfortable as possible.

- ઐ Allow yourself to feel a sense of safety for a few minutes.

- ઐ Then, gently start to open up your posture, opening up your arms and legs, your chest, your belly and your throat. You might want to stand up and open up your body as much as you can. Take your time throughout all of this process. With every breath you take, notice what it feels like to be more open with your body.

- ઐ Do you notice any feeling of vulnerability at any point in time? If so, where in your body do you notice it? What kind of sensation is it? Is it warm or cool? Is it throbbing or tingling? Does it feel like it's moving upwards or downwards, or is it immobile? If it had a shape or colour, what would it be? Are there any other things you notice about it?

- ઐ If at any point you start feeling a bit too vulnerable, contract your posture to one in which you were still feeling quite safe. Stay there for a while and then open your body up just a tiny bit more. How does it feel to do this?

- ઐ Write about your experience during this exercise. Focus on what it feels like for you to open up to vulnerability using your body.

13. Adopting a vulnerable posture

- ✎ Find a place where you know that you won't be disturbed.

- ✎ You can do this exercise by starting from four different postures: standing up, sitting down, lying down facing up or down, or on all fours. Whichever posture you take, allow it to be a neutral one with no tension in your body.

♊ Take a few breaths to get in touch with the feeling of safety while being in the posture you're in. Notice where you feel that sense of security in your body.

♊ Now, start opening up your body to a more vulnerable and exposed posture. Do this slowly, noticing changes in your emotions or body sensations and any thoughts that come to mind. Only take yourself as far as you want to. There's no shame in sticking to your limits. Adopt the gentle, nourishing approach of stretching out your comfort zone while only doing what feels safe for you.

♊ If you're standing up, put your hands behind your back and pull your elbows backwards. Widen the space between your feet as much as possible while still holding yourself strong. Pull your head backwards. Arch your back as far as is comfortable, ensuring that your chest is tilting upwards and that your pelvis is tilting backwards. Notice the feeling of vulnerability and exposure in your throat, armpits, chest, bum and inner thighs.

૪ If you're lying down, make your body take the form of an 'X' by pushing your arms upwards and outwards and your legs downwards and outwards. Spread your legs as wide as possible. If you're facing up, notice the feeling of vulnerability and exposure in your chest, belly, abdomen, genital area, inner thighs and the soles of your feet. If you're facing down, you can also arch your back and tilt your hip backwards so that your bum is pushing upwards. Notice the feeling of vulnerability and exposure in your neck, upper back, sides, lower back, bum, inner thighs and the soles of your feet.

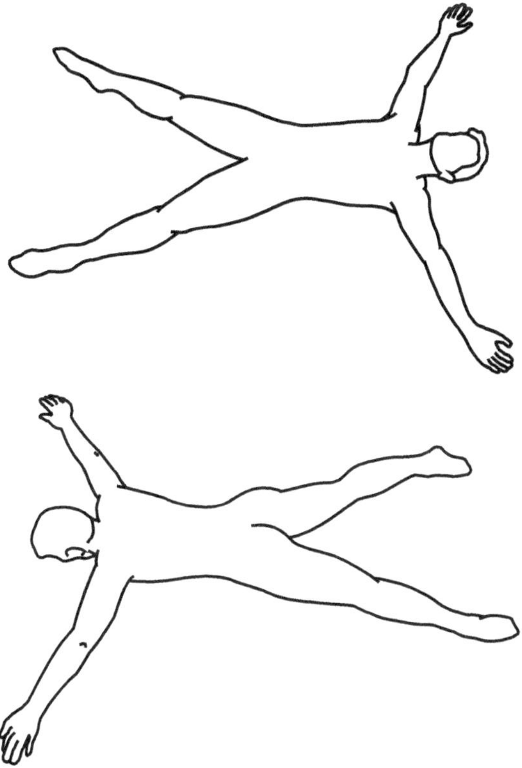

∽ If you're sitting down, push your shoulders back. Pull your arms downwards, outwards and backwards. Pull your head backwards. Open your legs as much as you can and have your feet pointing outwards. Notice the feeling of vulnerability and exposure in your throat, chest, belly, abdomen, genital area and inner thighs.

∽ If you're on all fours, lower yourself onto your elbows if it feels physically comfortable, keeping your forearms pointing towards the front with your hands open. Keep your head lowered down almost touching the surface you're on. Spread your knees as wide as is comfortable. Gently start arching your back, tilting your bum outwards and upwards. Notice the feeling of vulnerability and exposure in the soles of your feet, the back of your thighs, your bum, lower back, neck and the back of your head. Pay particular attention to the area around your anus as this posture tends to expose the skin around it which can trigger strong feelings of vulnerability and shame and can push you to close up again.

- ✖ Stay in this position for some time, noticing how it feels to be in a physically more exposed posture. In which parts of your body do you feel most vulnerable?

- ✖ If you feel comfortable, close your eyes. How does this alter the experience of vulnerability?

- ✖ Try reconnecting to the sense of security that you were feeling at the beginning of the exercise. Breathe deeply, connecting to that sense of security while keeping yourself in the physically exposed posture you're in. What do you notice about your emotions or body sensations?

- ✖ Finally, come back to a relaxed and comforting position. Take some time to reflect on what the process of opening up and adopting a vulnerable position with your body felt like and any thoughts, emotions or body sensations that were triggered. Was there any moment when you wanted to close up again? What did you do in that case?

- ✖ If you feel comfortable doing so, repeat the exercise while being naked or wearing the least amount of clothing you feel comfortable with. This can intensify the feeling of vulnerability so only go as far as is comfortable for you. Focus on how your emotions, thoughts and body sensations change throughout the exercise. In the end, notice what difference it made to do the exercise naked or wearing less clothing. If you chose not to repeat it naked or wearing less clothing, what stopped you?

❧ Write down your reflections about the exercise and what you learnt about yourself.

14. Being vulnerable in front of another

- Look back at exercises 12 and 13. If it's possible and you feel comfortable doing so, repeat them while in the presence of someone you trust.

- Notice what it feels like to be curled up in front of the other person. How does it feel to open up in front of someone else? How do your emotions, thoughts and body sensations change as you open up while being watched by someone else?

- If possible, consider doing the exercises in front of the other person while you're naked or wearing the least amount of clothing. Only go as far as you feel comfortable because being exposed in front of someone else can evoke stronger emotions. Notice the changes in your emotions, thoughts and body sensations as you open up while being in this more exposed state. How does wearing less clothing change your experience in comparison to before?

- If you chose not to repeat the exercise in front of someone else, try imagining it instead. Notice what feelings, thoughts and body sensations come up for you. Be honest with yourself – there's no thought, emotion or sensation to be ashamed of.

- In the end, reflect on your experience during this exercise. Focus on the experience of being watched in your vulnerability and how your body and emotions react to that, as well as the experience of being watched in a more exposed state.

15

ON SELF-ESTEEM

No human is an island. We're made to be in a group. It's something that's deeply wired into our biology, that of our ancestors and that of other apes. We are social beings. Our survival depends on our interactions with others in our group and the central element of this interaction is trust.

Our ancestors needed to know that they could trust each other, that the group would have their back when confronting dangerous situations, that when they went out hunting, those that remained behind would protect the children. They lived in small groups and knew the others in the group personally, meaning that they had the chance to develop that trust. If there were untrustworthy group members, they would no longer be welcome in the group and losing one's group jeopardised one's survival. So, members of the group would spend time and energy gaining each other's trust and approval in order to be held in good esteem by the group.

Audio files for this chapter can be accessed at
thehorsesmouth.michaelconti.net/lbwy-ch15
or by scanning the adjacent QR code.

Although nowadays we live in very differently structured societies, the need to be part of a group is still there. We still need to know that we can trust others in our family, peer group and immediate circles. We still need their approval and we often look for it. We still want them to see us in a positive light, earn their trust and be part of their group. This gives us a strong feeling of security.

The process of interacting with others in order to be part of a group is something we learn from when we're born. As babies or toddlers, we're completely vulnerable and so we need our parents or significant adults to keep us in their group, to look at us favourably. So, we try to please them in order to get their approval and acceptance. We also seek our siblings' approval, that of our teachers and of our peers. And we constantly monitor whether they're satisfied with us, often interpreting this as indicating something about us, about whether we're good enough to be liked and accepted.

Positive self-esteem

If we receive the message that we're likeable, we progressively internalise the message – we make it ours. We start believing that we're pleasant to be with. By time, this becomes our fundamental belief about ourselves and it offers us the security needed to be even more ourselves. As a result, we develop positive self-esteem and see ourselves in a positive light. We become more able to accept our flaws without seeing them as a threat to our self-worth, our relationship to others and, hence, our survival. We know that we're OK – warts and all.

Negative self-esteem

Although some people develop positive self-esteem, this isn't everybody's experience. Diverse life experiences teach us different things about ourselves. If the demands, expectations or the stress we experience are too high, we might judge ourselves as inadequate. If this becomes a repetitive thing, we internalise this message and start believing that we're not good enough. We start focusing too much on our flaws, judging them as bigger than they actually are. We start comparing ourselves with others and judging ourselves as inferior. We develop low self-esteem.

But what contributes to developing negative self-esteem? One major thing is having had very critical or disapproving parents, caregivers, siblings, peers or teachers when we were young. Another thing is having struggled a lot in our performance at school or having been bullied. We might have grown up in a religious environment that put a lot of emphasis on sin, where we saw everything as being either completely good or completely bad and promoted feelings of guilt, shame and self-loathing. The culture we live in and the media also teach us what kind of person we should be in order to be liked and they depict the consequences of not being such a person. We might have experienced physical, sexual or psychological abuse or neglect by parents, caregivers or partners. Or perhaps we experienced a long period of stressful events, such as a relationship breakdown, an ongoing medical condition or longer periods of anxiety or depression. All of these things might have taught us that there's something we're lacking in and we end up blaming the only one we think could be responsible for this: ourselves.

Low self-esteem can manifest in different ways. It can take the form of an inferiority complex. In this case, we give ourselves negative labels, such as 'incompetent' or 'unattractive'. We engage in negative talk with ourselves, telling ourselves things like "I'm so stupid!" or "I'm so ugly!" We blame ourselves when things go wrong while believing that achievements are mainly due to luck. We find it hard to believe compliments, always finding a 'but' to counteract them. At times, we might even tolerate unacceptable and abusive behaviour in our relationships. Or we might develop eating disorders or addictive behaviours which, in turn, act as a confirmation that we're not good enough. We live our lives in constant fear of judgement, always finding ourselves lacking in something and striving to get positive approval from others. We stop trying out new things, we avoid challenges and we focus our energies on not making mistakes rather than on growing and developing. In this way, we feel safer.

There are, however, some people who go through similar situations but react in the opposite way. When they sense the possibility of feeling inadequate, they put all their energy into avoiding feeling that. Instead of putting themselves down and feeling worthless, they overcompensate and develop a superiority complex. This isn't the same as being self-confident. Self-confidence is about perceiving ourselves realistically, feeling secure in ourselves despite our flaws. Instead, a superiority complex tries to suppress any manifestation or awareness of our flaws as this makes us feel insecure and vulnerable to rejection. We create an inflated image of ourselves that, unfortunately, we end up believing. We feel that we're better than others, develop a sense of entitlement, are unwilling to listen to others and any sort of criticism and have a hard time owning up to our mistakes. We tend to turn any situation into one that's about us, constantly seeking validation from others and putting others down in order to feel better about ourselves. It's also possible that we become perfectionists, believing that we're likeable and worthy only by being and acting perfectly. The result is that we set ourselves up for failure as there will always be higher expectations that we never reach. In the process, we end up displacing our frustrations and anger onto others or expecting them to also reach impossible standards.

Having an inferiority or superiority complex are two extremes of having low self-esteem. Some people are at either end of the spectrum and develop a personality based on that. However, the majority of us lie somewhere in between. This means that, while in some aspects of our life we feel OK about ourselves, in others we feel that we're not good enough and either put ourselves down or overcompensate for our sense of deficiency. Developing as a person implies nurturing our self-esteem in such a way that we see ourselves for who we truly are and accept our flaws without judging ourselves according to other people's expectations.

How to develop your self-esteem

The following are some suggestions to help nurture your self-esteem if your tendency leans more towards an inferiority complex.

- Start getting to know your positive qualities in a way that's not distorted by your negative judgements. You can also ask others to give you a more objective evaluation of yourself.

- Monitor how you talk negatively to yourself and start changing these statements to more positive ones.

- When you make a mistake, ask yourself how you can learn from it rather than using it to judge or punish yourself.

❧   Set challenges for yourself and engage fully in them. Step out of your comfort zone and notice that you can actually succeed in doing so.

❧   Schedule enjoyable activities for yourself on a regular basis. Pleasure helps us feel better about ourselves.

❧   Develop relationships with people who help you feel good about yourself and challenge you to grow, and avoid engaging with those who primarily make you feel bad about yourself.

❧   Get in touch with your needs, wants and feelings. Communicate them directly and honestly to others.

❧   Learn to say "No!" It will make you feel stronger and more confident.

The following suggestions can be of help if your tendency leans more towards a superiority complex.

❧   When you find yourself judging others, check with yourself how this is linked to a sense of insecurity you have about yourself. For example, are you judging others as ugly because you feel insecure about your own appearance?

❧   When you find yourself criticising others, stop and think about whether such criticism is warranted. If it is, ensure you give more genuine praise than criticism.

The following exercises aim at helping you deepen your awareness of your sense of worth and understand what contributes to it. They also offer you an opportunity to work through your self-judgements and, in doing so, further develop your self-esteem.

How it relates to your life

How does this text relate to your life?
Write down anything that comes to mind, heart or body.

Exercises

01. Me on the page

৬ Find some crayons or coloured pens. In the space below, draw yourself. Use as much space or colour as you want to. The aim isn't to create a work of art – even a stick figure will do!

Me!

৶   Look back at your drawing and reflect on the following:

  ♦   How much space did you occupy on the page and how much empty space did you leave around you?

  ♦   Did you use colour when drawing yourself?

  ♦   Did you draw any face and, if so, what facial expression did you draw?

  ♦   Is there something that you want to change in your drawing to better reflect how you see yourself? If so, modify the drawing.

৶   Look at the final drawing and write down your interpretation of what it shows you about how you see yourself.

02. Rating myself

⚘ Go through the following list. Using a scale of -5 (completely bad/incompetent) to +5 (completely good/competent), mark how good you feel about yourself in that specific area. In the end, add up your scores.

	How good I feel about myself (-5 to +5)
My intellectual ability	
My level of creativity	
My level of self-awareness	
My intuitive ability, my gut feelings	
My ability to be social and connect with others	
My ability to connect with my emotions and those of others	
My physical appearance	
My level of awareness of, and connection with, my body	
My sex life	
Final score (out of a maximum of -45 or +45):	

⚘ Look at the different scores and write down what they indicate about how much you value yourself. Are there any areas you would like to develop more self-esteem in?

03. Justifying my low ratings

Look back at exercise 02 and choose the three or four areas you rated yourself the lowest in. For each one of them, use the table below to list one or two reasons why you think you see yourself in that way.

Area of life	Reasons for giving a low rating

§ Write down what you've learnt about why you see yourself in the way you do. Avoid writing in a blaming tone – be compassionate with yourself when writing.

04. Comparing myself to others

- ✍ Look back at the list in exercise 02.

- ✍ Look at those areas where you think lowly of yourself. Who do you compare yourself to when it comes to these things? Who do you think excels the most in those areas?

- ✍ Now, look at those areas where you tend to think highly of yourself. Who do you believe struggles the most in those areas?

Area of life	I am worse than ...	I am better than ...
My intellectual ability		
My level of creativity		
My level of self-awareness		
My intuitive ability, my gut feelings		
My ability to be social and connect with others		
My ability to connect with my emotions and those of others		
My physical appearance		
My level of awareness of, and connection with, my body		
My sex life		

- ❧ Go through the names of the people you've just listed and try answering the following questions:
  - How much do you really know that person?
  - Are they excellent or a failure in all areas of life?
  - What does this tell you about the different qualities that make up a person and how you evaluate them?
  - What does this tell you about how you judge yourself in relation to others?
- ❧ Write down your reflections in the space below.

05. Physically locating my self-worth

- Stand or sit in front of a mirror or a photo of yourself and close your eyes.

- Focus on your breathing and notice any sensations in your body.

- Now, open your eyes and spend a few minutes looking at yourself. Observe if you experience any changes in your body sensations.

- Try to find the place in your body where you feel that your sense of self-worth is primarily located. Is it a pleasant or an unpleasant sensation? What does it feel like?

- Write down what you've learnt about how your self-worth is present in your body.

06. Embodying my self-esteem

- Find a space where you're undisturbed and where you can stretch in all directions without hitting anything.

- Stand up straight and close your eyes. Think of your self-esteem – how you feel about, and judge, yourself. Notice where in your body you feel your self-esteem.

- Take a few deeper breaths, imagining that the air you inhale is reaching this part of your body in order to better connect to it.

- Now, allow your body to take a posture that better reflects your self-esteem. It may be a static posture or it may include movement. Check in with your posture a lot of times to see if you need to modify it to better mirror your self-esteem.

- Stay in this posture for a few minutes, noticing what it feels like to be embodying your self-esteem and any emotions that come up for you.

- In the end, come back to a relaxed posture and reflect on how it felt to be in that posture. What more did you learn in relation to how you feel about yourself? Is there anything you would want to change?

- Write down what you learnt about yourself and how you embody your self-esteem.

____

____

____

____

____

____

____

____

07. When I feel bad about myself

- ❧ Recall the last time you felt bad about yourself and experienced a sense of inferiority. Focus on what you wanted or needed at that moment and any thoughts or emotions you experienced. Write them down in the table below.

- ❧ Repeat this whenever you experience something similar.

Brief description of the experience	What I wanted or needed	What I felt	What I thought
e.g. A friend forgot to turn up for a meeting we had planned.	I wanted my friend to come rushing to meet me and apologise.	I felt betrayed, abandoned and of no value.	This really confirms that my friends are not interested in me.

∾ Look back at your experiences. Do you observe any patterns? Write down your observations about your reactions in the space below.

____

____

____

____

____

____

____

____

____

____

____

____

____

____

____

08. People in my life

- Use the table below to list people who are quite significant in your life, both in a good or a bad way. Include parents or caregivers, siblings, other family members, your partner, boyfriend or girlfriend, work colleagues and friends. Write their names down in the first column.

- Go through the list and think about how being with each person makes you feel about yourself and how it affects your self-esteem.

- Using a scale of -5 (very negative) to +5 (very positive), rate how you feel about yourself when you're with that person.

Person	Rating (-5 to +5)

09. Plotting self-esteem across my lifespan

The horizontal line below represents your life. Use the space above and below this line to sketch another line that represents how your self-esteem changed during your lifetime. The further up you go on the graph, the more you followed the 'should' statements. The further down you go, the more you opposed them. If there was a significant rise or fall, can you identify what was happening during that moment in your life? Write it down on the graph.

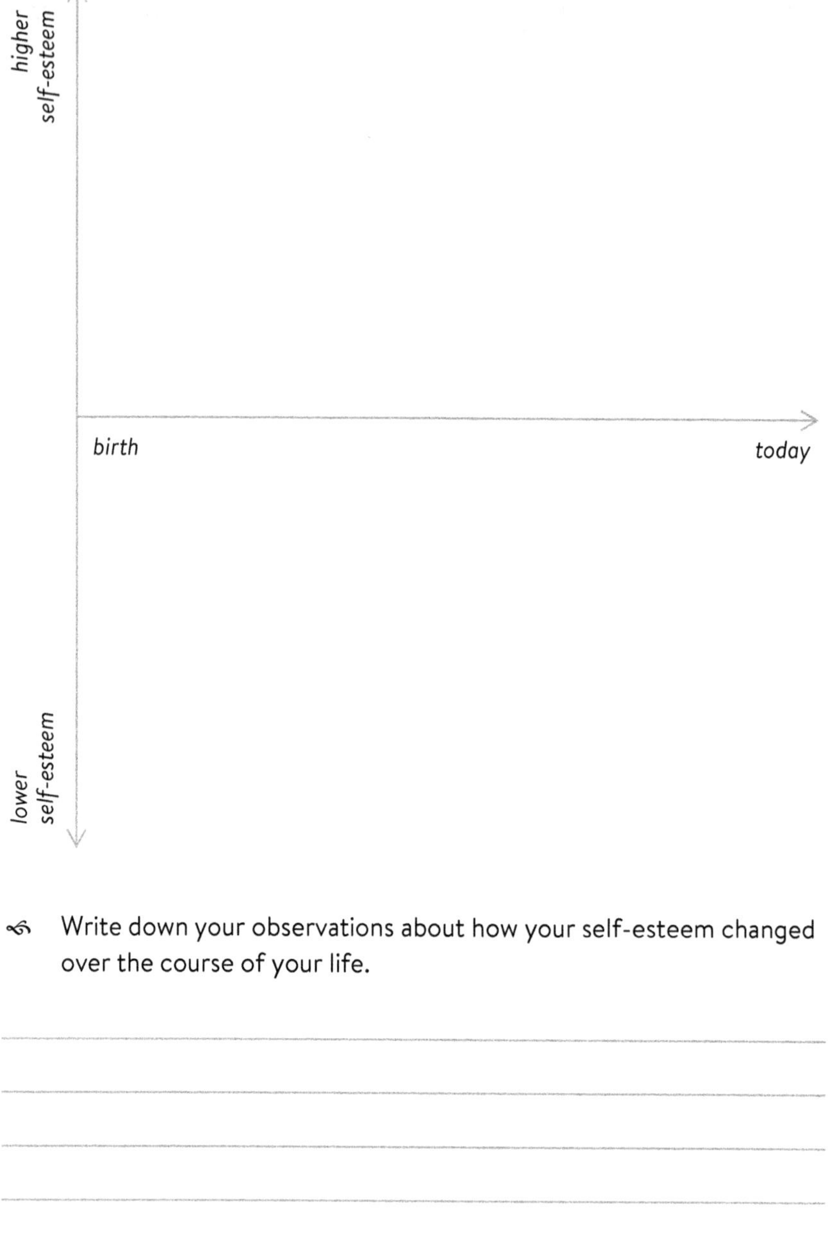

✍ Write down your observations about how your self-esteem changed over the course of your life.

____

____

____

____

____

____

____

10. Contributors to low self-esteem

✍ Go through the following list and tick which ones were present in your life.

	Present in my life
Very critical or disapproving parents or caregivers	
Very critical or disapproving siblings	
Very critical or disapproving teachers	
Very critical or disapproving peers	
Abusive or neglectful parents, caregivers or significant adults	
Bullying	
Low performance at school	
Critical or shaming religious beliefs	
Media messages about being beautiful and cool	
Ongoing stressful events	
Ongoing medical condition	
A mental health condition (e.g. anxiety or depression)	
Other traumatic situations	

- ✎ Which of the things that were present in your life do you think had the most negative impact on how you value yourself?
- ✎ Think about whether there were other things that negatively impacted your self-esteem and write them down in the space below.
- ✎ Write down what you learnt about how your self-worth was affected by each of these circumstances.

11. Choosing my company

∽ Look back at exercise 08. Who are the people who make you feel good about yourself? Who are those who make you feel bad about yourself? Write down who they are below and feel free to add others.

People who make me feel good about myself	People who make me feel bad about myself

∽ Make a clear resolution to spend more time with the group of people who have your best interests at heart and make you feel good about yourself, and to reduce considerably the amount of time you spend with those who primarily make you feel bad about yourself.

12. Nine good things about me

- Ask three of the people who are closest to you to each tell you three good qualities about yourself. Write them down in the table below.

Person	Qualities they say I have
	1. 2. 3.
	1. 2. 3.
	1. 2. 3.

- Now, stand or sit in front of a mirror.
- While looking at yourself and maintaining eye contact, bring to mind the first quality that you wrote down.
- Say it aloud to yourself in the form: "I am [the quality] ."
- Notice any emotions or body sensations that come up for you. Notice if you start thinking about how this is not true. Every time you notice this, repeat the phrase aloud again. Feel free to increase the volume of your voice to make it sound more affirming.

❧ Note down how it feels to allow yourself to accept positive qualities about yourself that others see in you.

13. The impression others have of me

- Think of people in your life who have a good impression of you. Use the table below to make a list of these people and write down what you think their impression of you is. Try summing it up in a sentence or two.

- You might want to check with them what you wrote and maybe add new things that they mention.

Person	Their impression of me

֎ Now, cut out some paper cards, the size of a bank card. You might want to use thicker paper that's more durable. On each card, write down one of the statements and the name of the person.

֎ Carry the cards around with you in your wallet or bag. Every time you notice that you're feeling bad about yourself, look at one of them and imagine that person saying that thing about you.

14. Being held with love

֎ Find a quiet place and sit comfortably.

֎ Play some beautiful music. You might want to burn some incense or use an essential oil that you particularly like.

֎ Imagine that one of the people from exercise 13 is there with you. Close your eyes and hold yourself in a hugging posture.

֎ Be aware of the sensation of being held. Imagine that it's them who are embracing you. Imagine them telling you what they think of you, how they perceive you and the positive impressions that they have of you.

֎ Notice what emotions come up for you and what you sense in your body as you allow yourself to listen to them and be held by them.

- ❧ If possible, repeat this exercise with an actual person, asking them to tell you what they think of you while physically embracing you.
- ❧ Write about your experience of being held and spoken to in a loving and affirming way. Take note of the changes this brings about in your emotions and body sensations.

15. Positive qualities

- ❧ Use the space below to make a list of your positive qualities in the form: 'I am [quality] .'

I am
I am
I am

I am
I am
I am
I am
I am
I am
I am
I am

- Pick one of the qualities and write it down on a large sheet of paper. Place it somewhere prominent where you live or work. Every time you see it, repeat that statement aloud to yourself. Leave it there for a whole week.

- The following week, pick another statement and repeat the exercise.

- At the end of each week, ask yourself how you feel about yourself in relation to that quality. Write down your observations in the table below.

My positive quality	Observations at the end of the week

My positive quality	Observations at the end of the week

16. A letter to myself

- Look at the list of positive qualities in exercise 15 and see if you want to add any new ones.

- Use the space below or another sheet of paper to write a letter to yourself, focusing explicitly on these qualities and how they're present in your life. Maybe you can remind yourself of one or two situations that illustrate each of the qualities. As much as possible, ensure that you have a paper copy so you can carry it around with you if you want to.

17. Learning from my mistakes

❧ When you make a mistake and notice that you're criticising yourself, ask yourself what you can learn from the situation and how you can do things differently.

❧ Note down your mistakes and what you've learnt from them in the table below. Make sure that you phrase this learning in a loving and non-judgemental way towards yourself.

The situation	What I learnt

<table>
<tr><td></td><td></td></tr>
<tr><td></td><td></td></tr>
</table>

18. Moving between extremes

- Find a space where you're undisturbed and where you can stretch out in all directions without hitting anything.

- Stand up straight and close your eyes. Think about how you feel about yourself, noticing where you are feeling these emotions in your body.

- Take a few deeper breaths imagining that the air is reaching this part of your body.

- After a few breaths, allow your body to take a posture that better reflects how you feel about yourself. It may be a static posture or it may include movement. Check in with your posture and see if you can modify it to better mirror your sense of self-worth.

- After a couple of minutes, start changing your posture to make it feel like you're amplifying your sense of self-worth. Make yourself even more inferior or superior, depending on how much self-esteem you feel that you have.

- Stay in this posture for a few minutes. Notice what it feels like emotionally and in your body to be in that position.

- Now, start moving your body to a posture that would reflect the opposite level of self-esteem. If you're in a posture reflecting low self-esteem, adopt one of superiority and pride, and vice versa.

- Stay in this posture for a few minutes. Notice how it feels emotionally and in your body to be in this new posture.

- Now, allow your body to move in such a way as to find a position between the two extremes. Check in with your body as many times as necessary until you feel that you've reached the posture that feels best for you.
- Spend some time in this posture and notice how it feels to be there.
- Write down what you noticed about the experience of using your body to reflect your self-esteem and its opposite and what it feels like to embody the in-between.

19. From apology to gratitude

- ⤷ During the coming week, use the table below to note down when you apologise to others and why you do that.

- ⤷ At the end of each day, go over your apologies and note down whether or not your apology was needed or whether you ended up apologising even when you didn't do anything wrong.

- ⤷ For each time that you apologised when you didn't need to, ask yourself what you could have been grateful for instead. Write this down in the third column.

The situation I apologised in	Was the apology needed? Why?	What gratitude could I have shown instead?
e.g. I told my partner about something that I was uncomfortable about and my partner was a bit upset about it.	*I didn't need to apologise because I was expressing how things affected me and wasn't intentionally hurting my partner.*	*I could have shown my gratitude towards my partner for listening to my concerns and being interested in our relationship.*

The situation	Apology needed?	Possible gratitude

- During the following week, try to notice when you're about to apologise. Unless you've done something wrong, turn it into a statement of gratitude. For example, if you arrive 5 minutes later than someone else for an appointment and the other person was already waiting, instead of saying "Sorry for having to wait", say, "Thank you for waiting."

20. My bucket list

- Make a list of things that you wish to do in your life, including some challenging ones.
- Rate each one of them on a scale of difficulty where 1 is the easiest to accomplish and 10 is the most difficult.
- Pick the easiest one and choose a date and place to do it.

❧ Before you engage in the experience, check what your level of self-worth is at that moment. After your experience, check it again and notice if there's been any shift in how you perceive yourself.

Activity	Date and place	How I see myself (before)	How I see myself (after)

ᔕ Write down what you learnt about how achieving different things impacts your sense of worth.

____

____

____

____

____

____

____

____

____

____

____

____

____

21. Saying "No!"

ᔕ Find a space where you won't be disturbed and where no one can hear you.

ᔕ Try doing this exercise while standing up with your eyes closed.

ᔕ Imagine the last time that you said "Yes!" to someone when you didn't want to. Picture the situation.

ᔕ Start breathing more deeply. Allow your breath to reach your lower abdomen, all the way down to your perineum, the area between the genitals and the anus.

ᔕ With every exhale, imagine that you're saying "No!" instead.

- When you feel ready, scream out loud your "No!" with all your strength. Feel free to move your body in any way that's helpful so you can let out that "No!"
- Let yourself calm down and re-centre yourself in the standing position. Allow your breathing to come back to normal.
- Picture the situation again and check if there's any desire to say "No!" again. If so, repeat the process.
- In the end, use your arms to embrace yourself as illustrated in exercise 14. Compliment yourself aloud for having allowed yourself to stand your ground and say "No!"
- Notice what you're feeling in your body and any emotions that you're experiencing.
- Write about your experience during this exercise. How does it feel to say "No!" and how can this help you feel better about yourself?

22. Positively noticing others (for those with a superiority complex)

- If you tend to feel a sense of superiority in relation to others, go back to exercise 04 and look at the areas where you believe you're better in comparison to others.

- Pick one area and write it down in the table below. During the coming week, focus only on this area.

- Notice how others are also good at that thing. Every time you notice someone being good in that area, speak aloud and say to yourself: "[name of person] is also good at [the thing] ."

- Take note of any emotions or body sensations you experience in relation to this. Then, continue with your day. Be aware that you might find yourself strongly resisting the exercise in the first place!

- During the following weeks, repeat this exercise with other areas that you indicated in exercise 04.

	Area you believe you're better in
Week 1	
Week 2	
Week 3	
Week 4	
Week 5	
Week 6	

- Write down what you've learnt about yourself during this exercise and about how others might also be as good as you are. Take note of what emotions or body sensations this triggered in you.

23. Praising others
(for those with a superiority complex)

- ✍ Be on the lookout for when you criticise someone else. When you catch yourself doing so, ensure that you also genuinely praise them for two other qualities they have.

- ✍ Check in with your emotions and body sensations when you do so. What thoughts come to mind? If you find yourself criticising the other person in your mind, find more qualities to praise them for.

- Focus on the other person's reactions when you're praising them. In what way does this improve the interaction between both of you?
- Write down what emotions and body sensations you experienced when engaging with others in this manner. What did you notice about the other people's reactions and how your interaction changed? What can you learn from this exercise about how to interact better with others?

ABOUT THE AUTHOR

Michael Conti is a highly qualified and experienced psychotherapist, trauma specialist, coach, counsellor and supervisor for psychosocial professionals.

Michael started off his education in Malta as a science teacher. He then moved to Italy where he worked in the social sector and later moved to France to complete his studies in philosophy. Following this, he read for a Master's degree in Integrative Counselling and Psychotherapy in the United Kingdom and later furthered his education with another Master's degree in Supervision for Psychosocial Professionals.

In his many years of experience, he has worked in different settings, including LGBTQIA+ organisations, schools, vocational colleges, emergency services and private practice. During his work as a deputy head of service at the London Fire Brigade (UK) he specialised in working with psychological trauma and trained as an EMDR therapist. Michael also undertook an education as a specialist in Somatic Sexuality (ICS) in Spain and is the founder of Orange Bodies, an initiative where he works with embodiment practice.

In addition, he has taught on Master's degree programmes, published in journals and delivered seminars, workshops and trainings to both professionals and organisations.

www.ingramcontent.com/pod-product-compliance
Lightning Source LLC
LaVergne TN
LVHW010308200726
843507LV00010B/1195